MUSIC

MUSIC

Selected Poems

Tarō Naka

translated by

Andrew Houwen

&

Chikako Nihei

ISOBAR
PRESS

First published in 2018 by

Isobar Press
Sakura 2-21-23-202, Setagaya-ku,
Tokyo 156-0053, Japan
&
14 Isokon Flats, Lawn Road,
London NW3 2XD, United Kingdom

http://isobarpress.com

ISBN 978-4-907359-23-2

ACKNOWLEDGEMENTS
Some of the translations, or earlier versions of them, have
previously appeared in the following publications or online jour-
nals, to whose editors grateful thanks are offered: *Asian Cha*,
Modern Poetry in Translation, *Poetry Salzburg Review*, *Shearsman*,
Tears in the Fence, and *Tokyo Poetry Journal*.

IMAGES
Front cover: *August 1, 2014*, copyright © Matsumoto Hiroshi,
2014. Author photograph courtesy of the *Asahi Shimbun* news-
paper; photograph of the nō stage on page 96 courtesy of the
National Noh Theatre of Japan.

Further acknowledgements appear on page 137.

CONTENTS

A NOTE ON NAMES

Throughout the book names of Japanese people appear in Japanese order with the surname first, except in the case of the cover and title page – where Naka's name appears in the English order – and in mentions of Japanese authors who publish primarily in English.

INTRODUCTION

Naka Tarō is one of the most highly respected poets in post-war Japan. Compared with Ibaragi Noriko and Tanikawa Shuntarō, however, whose poems have often featured on television and in school examinations, he is more of a poets' poet. His *oeuvre* reflects his life-long exploration of Buddhism, traditional and modern literature, language, art, and philosophy. Although he was raised in a post-war poetic climate that distrusted the calling of attention to the materiality of words, he developed a poetics, rooted in his profound knowledge of traditional Japanese poetry, that paid attention to the interaction between what he described as the visual, phonetic, and historical aspects of words. He thus saw each word as a unique 'thing' rather than a sign that merely points to what it signifies; consequently, he felt the translation of poetry that took all these aspects into consideration to be 'impossible'. For this reason, perhaps, he has not yet achieved the recognition abroad that he deserves, despite the acclaim he has received in Japan, where he was awarded the Yomiuri, Murō Saisei, Contemporary Poets, Tōson Memorial, and Japanese Arts Academy Prizes.

My co-translator Chikako Nihei and I have sought to respect the methods of his poetry by trying to consider the interaction of the aspects of words listed above; but we also recognise, as Naka does, that a poem always changes with each new reader. In Naka's case, this recognition stems from his Buddhist understanding of all things' impermanence. A poem is therefore also impermanent: the reader, he writes in his 'Notes for a Poetics' of 1966, 'always creates the work as a new phenomenon'. The same can be said for a poem's translators. A number of English versions of Naka's poems have appeared in magazines and anthologies, each recreating them in a different way. This is, however, his first collection in English. It presents a selection of poems from across his poetic output, as well as his nō play, *The First Emperor,* and his 'Notes for a Poetics'.

Naka was born Fukuda Shōjirō on 23 January 1922 in Hakata, part of the city of Fukuoka on the island of Kyūshū in western Japan. (His pen-name derives from Naka Ward in Hakata.) It was during his second year at Fukuoka Middle School that he began reading the poetry of Hagiwara Sakutarō, who was arguably the most prominent Japanese poet of the early twentieth century and played an important role in introducing free verse into Japanese. As a Fukuoka High School student, he also read writers as diverse as Nietzsche, Dostoevsky, Mann, Baudelaire, and the Kyoto School philosopher Nishida Kitarō. In April 1941, months before Pearl Harbour, he entered Tokyo Imperial University to study Japanese Literature. One of his earliest poems, 'Street Scene', evokes the tense silences of everyday life in a country at war – 'not even the sound of footsteps on the pavement / the shutters drawn down over all the windows' – while the war rages somewhere out of sight, across the ocean:

> beyond the zinc roofs the endlessly open sea
> on a tower an unseen flag flutters

On 1 October 1943, at the age of twenty-one, he was called up to serve in the Japanese navy; he never experienced frontline action, however, as he was assigned a job teaching Japanese at the Imperial Japanese Naval Academy in Tokyo. A selection of his earliest poems, including 'Street Scene', appeared in his first collection, *Etudes*, brought out in an edition of five hundred copies in 1950 by his former Fukuoka High School classmate, Date Tokuo.

More poems appeared in two anthologies brought out by Date's Eureka press: *Sengo shijin zenshū* ('Anthology of Post-War Poets', 1954) and *Gendai shijin zenshū* ('Anthology of Contemporary Poets', 1959). In these poems, Naka's interest in Buddhism is already apparent. The critic Hirai Shōbin recalls that Naka would often recite the *Heart Sutra*. Naka came to realise the importance of its emphasis on the impermanence of all things when confronted with the war's destruction. 'Scene 11', for instance, recalls the dropping of the atomic bombs on Hiroshima and Nagasaki:

> pushed along in the flow
> countless burnt eyes
> eyes
> eyes

War-time experience coincides here with Buddhist thought: the 'burnt eyes' and the 'collapsed temple's hollowed eye-sockets' resulting from the nuclear explosion are also the eyes on fire in the sutra known in English as the 'Fire Sermon', in which the Buddha tells his followers that 'All things are on fire [...] the eye, O priests, is on fire; forms are on fire; eye-consciousness is on fire'. When Naka returned to Hakata after the war, he found that his home, and his hometown, had been devastated. The visceral impact of this trauma is evident in many of his poems from this period.

Facing the 'rubble' of the Japanese post-war landscape, the speaker of 'Scene 111' concludes that 'life has no direction' as he moves through a town 'fallen to pieces but starting to rebuild':

> leaning on the rusty railing of distrust   I smoke cheap
> Golden Bat
>
> the root and purpose of existence   out of sight already
> long ago

Naka's indebtedness to Baudelaire during this phase of his poetic development is evident in the explicit statement of what the 'rusty railing' symbolises. A subtler approach can be detected, however, in his reference to 'Golden Bat', a brand of cigarette then popular with hard-up artists. It suggests the analogy Naka uses for impermanence in his 1947 essay 'The Road': when relating his reaction to what had happened in the war, he describes his 'fear' of the 'emptiness' that accompanied a loss of the values that had seemed so certain; this was like 'the moment of noticing the smoke vanishing before your eyes when smoking a cigarette'. In the same essay, he states his belief that there are only 'bare appearances' without purpose. The speaker of 'Scene III' likewise not only finds that there is no 'root and purpose of existence'; he also discovers its 'infinite absence'.

Beginning with some of the poems published in the *Anthology of Contemporary Poets,* however, Naka's approach to such 'bare appearances' changes. 'Autumn Walk' contrasts with poems such as 'Scene II' and 'Scene III' through its emphasis on poetic creation: the poet 'skilfully pulls up fine words like radishes'. The comparison between physical things and words is pursued throughout the poem. Rather than denying or lamenting the gap between the two, the poem accepts it: 'the word stone is another, separate thing / from the physical stone'. Words are no less 'things' than physical things and 'infinitely modulate / in the organic connections of their world'. In his conception of words as 'things', Naka was influenced by Sartre's famous assertion in *What is Literature?* of 1948 that the poet 'has chosen the poetic attitude which considers words as things and not as signs'. The poem follows what the words do to one another, rather than the words following the poem's conception. This foreshadows Naka's *Shiron no tame no nōto* ('Notes for a Poetics', 1966) in which he states that 'To seek the autonomous order of words themselves as "things"' is 'what the writer of poetry follows as he creates'.

Music likewise takes on an important significance in 'Autumn Walk'. It is also the music of the natural world: 'the withered leaves of the sweetcorn rustle, *saya saya* / its music is deeper than autumn'. The poem concludes:

> a painting is more existence-like than existence
> but music goes beyond it towards infinity

thus the transparent sky is filled with music
scattering withered leaves and leaves of speech
all life vanishes in that direction

Naka's heavy use of abstraction here again suggests the relative immaturity of his poetry at this time; nevertheless, the poem's ending serves as an indication of the approach he was beginning to develop. The void, in this case the 'transparent sky', remains; but the plenitude of the 'music' offers a form of redress in a world where 'all life vanishes': the 'leaves' of both the natural world and that of words scatter. (In 'leaves of speech', *koto no ha*, Naka draws apart the two constituent elements of the Japanese for 'word', *kotoba*: 'speech', *koto*, and 'leaves', *ha*.) Instead of being merely resigned to this, however, 'Autumn Walk' marks a first step towards its celebration.

Music provides the theme for Naka's first mature collection, *Ongaku* ('Music'), which was composed between 1957 and 1964 and published in 1965 by Shichōsha, the foremost poetry publisher in post-war Japan, in a limited edition of four hundred copies. Hirai states that 'the more than twenty years' before *Music*'s publication 'were a preparation for this collection'. It received widespread critical praise, winning both the Yomiuri and Murō Saisei prizes, and is often considered Naka's *magnum opus*. Its importance within his *oeuvre*, together with the significance of music for his work, makes *Music* a suitable title for this translated collection.

At the end of *Music*, Naka appends a note on the Buddhist concept of *mu*, here translated as 'nothingness', even though '*mu*', Naka himself explains, 'is not "nothing". It is the *mu* of existing things, breathing *mu*, the *mu* of writhing waves'. In order to try and grasp this concept more fully, it is perhaps worth briefly discussing one or two of its Buddhist interpretations.

In the *Lotus Sutra*, a well-known text in Japan due to its importance for Tendai, the most widespread form of Buddhism in the country, Buddha tells his disciples that 'all phenomena are empty, that being their true identity': they are 'without innate nature' and it is 'only through causes and conditions that they exist'. In other words, there is no fundamental essence of any entity: each consists only of an agglomeration of parts from other entities, which themselves have no fundamental essence either. Our imagining of the world as consisting of discrete objects is, in this view, an illusion. As Naka adds, however, this does not mean that phenomena are entirely non-existent either: '*mu* is not "nothing"'. Illusions and dreams are not real; but their shapes or images do exist nonetheless. *Mu* is therefore not to be considered as a binary contrast with existence or as something elsewhere beyond it, but rather as something that pervades all existence. It is this non-dual understanding of *mu* that underlies the later *Heart Sutra*'s central claim: 'form is emptiness, emptiness is form'.

As this concept applies to all entities, it also applies to poetry. All things change from and into other things and have no permanent essence. As the seventh-century South Indian Buddhist thinker Candrakīrti (known in Japan as Gesshō) writes, 'the master and his work' are 'not the same'. Naka likewise connects the concept of *mu* with that of authorship:

> Through the action of creating, the creating subject is cut loose from what it has created. It allows the creation to exist on its own. It is itself always returned to *mu* [...] because words are created through the process of *mu*, they are not the possession of any particular individual'.

A poem, as a product of the combination of words, depends on the words' interaction with each other, which is something that, as Naka observes in 'Notes for a Poetics', 'always *surpasses* the writer' (Naka's emphasis); and, as words' associations continually shift with new readings, the poem, like all entities, is in constant flux. 'The reader', Naka writes, 'always creates the work as a new phenomenon. So the writer, too, after finishing writing, is just another reader'. While entities thus morph into and out of one another, the ceaselessly changing patterns they make are Naka's 'music'.

This approach and the poet's practice of following the 'autonomous order of words themselves' as derived from Sartre's *What is Literature?* informs 'Fautrier's Birds', the first poem in *Music* included in this collection. It is not an *ekphrasis* of an existing Jean Fautrier painting, although it bears some resemblance to *Enchevêtrements*, which was exhibited at the Tokyo Biennale in 1961. Instead, the fortuitous coincidence of additional meanings in the Japanese transcription of Fautrier's name in the poem's title, *'Fōtorie no tori'*, gives rise to the piece: the *'Fō'* in *'Fōtorie'* is the English 'four', while *'tori'* also means 'birds' and *'e'* painting in Japanese; thus, out of the name 'Fautrier', Naka conjures up a 'four birds painting'. The birds in the poem are 'endlessly emerging from themselves', yet 'never arriving / never stopping / at themselves' either. Like all entities, they are 'forever flying', never achieving a fixed identity. They thus come to represent a 'whirling world' in which everything is always becoming, never being.

At the start of the poem, the four birds are described thus: 'one bird green / one bird purple / two birds transparent'. The 'green' and 'purple' are at first chosen because of their alliteration in Japanese (*'midori'* and *'murasaki'*); but these colours then take on an added significance. Green is associated with growth and beginnings: it is a 'fresh bud at daybreak' and the 'predawn' gleam. Purple, meanwhile, is the 'flame of *mu*' (with a pun on the *mu* of *'murasaki'*) and the 'whip of *mu*' (punning on the *mu* of *'muchi'*, 'whip') that moves all things; it is thus connected with change and destruction. Together, they suggest the constant arising and fading away of all things in the cycle of death and rebirth. The choice of Matsumoto Hiroshi's painting for the cover of this book responded to this colour contrast's importance in illustrating Naka's conception of *mu*. The fortunate pun of the English 'music' on *mu* adds to the suitability of this collection's title.

In *Music* Naka also expands his investigation of words as 'things' rather than as mere signs pointing to something else. This is not to say that they defy the principle of *mu* stated above; rather, his investigation pays attention to how they, too, are each a unique combination of what Naka describes in 'Notes for a Poetics' as their 'visual', 'acoustic', and 'historical' aspects. He gives 石 (*ishi*, 'stone') as an example: it can be associated through its visual similarity as a Chinese character with 右 (*migi*, 'right', as opposed to left); through sound with *nishi* ('west'); or historically, with poems such as Bashō's haiku, *Ishiyama no ishi yori shiroshi aki no kaze* ('Whiter than the stones of Ishiyama Temple – the winds of autumn').

Naka's attention to the visual aspect of words partly relies on the Japanese language's use of Chinese characters. Most characters are composed of a relatively small number of more basic pictographic characters: for example, 好 ('good') consists of 女 ('woman') and 子 ('child'). The inclusion of such component characters indicates either semantic or phonetic information for the character in question. In 'Fautrier's Birds', for instance, the movement of the 'whirling world / turning time' (*senkai suru sekai / jiten suru jikan*) contains an implicit reference to the Japanese for the Buddhist *saṃsāra*, the cycle of death and rebirth (輪廻, *rinne*): the *'kai'* of *senkai* (回) means 'to turn' and can be found in the upper right-hand of the *'ne'* of *rinne* (廻), which also refers to turning. The *'ten'* of *jiten* (転) and the *'rin'* of *rinne* (輪), meanwhile, contain the element 車 (*kuruma*, 'vehicle'), which originally refers to a wheel. Both the visual and 'historical' aspects of these lines thus intersect.

Naka not only makes use of alliteration in exploring where such coincidences of sound take his poem; his choice of consonants at the conclusion of 'Fautrier's Birds' mimics the transition from the 'hard wind' (*katai kaze*) to the stillness of the 'predawn green's / wake' (*mimei no midori no / mio*):

katai kaze
uzumaku uta
ōkii obie no omoi ongaku
hateshinaku onore kara hazure zuretsutsu
tōku tori wa tonde yamanai
mu no murasaki no muchi
mimei no midori no
mio...

Perceptions of sounds' hardness or softness can differ between and within languages and cultures. In this case, a shift in these lines from hard to soft consonants is noted by Hirai:

> The music of this chain of alliteration gradually moves and diminishes to weak sounds, from *ka* to *mu* and *mi* [...][in the lines] *mimei no midori no / mio* ['the predawn green's / wake'], the light softens, the sound fades, the rhythm fades away.

Indeed, it is possible to observe how the 'large looming music' of the strong 'k'-sound alliteration in *katai kaze* ('solid wind') plays through the ensuing lines: *uzumaku* ('whirling'), *ōkii* ('large'), *ongaku* ('music'), *kara* ('from'), *tōku* ('distantly') and *murasaki* ('purple') all contain this consonant. This sound then fades out: four of the first five words quoted here contain 'k', then only one of the final fourteen. The 'm'-sounds, by contrast, increase: the first eighteen words contain two with 'm'; the last eleven contain seven. The poem's phonetic aspect thus interacts with the scene it evokes: the poem's consonant patterns also evoke the abatement of the 'solid wind'.

The title poem of Naka's next collection after *Music*, *Hakata*, which was published by Seidosha, a press affiliated with Date's poetry magazine *Eureka*, expands the approach of Naka's poetics in *Music*. The 'waves' that he uses as an example of *mu* in his 'Note on Mu' are connected in the poem with Buddhism through a play on *butsu*, which can mean both 'Buddha' and 'to beat' (as in 'beating waves'):

tearing waves'   buds of tears
namu namu Amida Buddha   buddha buddha
                                            beating beating

nadareru nami no   namida no tsubu no
nami nami amida butsu   butsu butsu butsu butsu

Waves are a frequent Buddhist metaphor for *mu* because they are an example of something which has no inherent existence. In Naka's Japanese, 'waves' (*nami*) plays on the 'tears' of crying (*namida*) to suggest the *lacrimae rerum* due to things lacking inherent existence; Chikako and I have attempted to replicate this in our use of 'tearing' to describe the waves' action. The 'buds' (*tsubu*) anticipate the *butsu* of 'buddha' / 'beating' by its sound proximity; fortunately, the English 'bud' can perform a similar function in relation to 'buddha'. '*Namu Amida Butsu*' ('Hail Amida Buddha') is the invocation of Amida Buddha, to whose 'Pure Land' people pass away in many forms of Tendai Buddhism. Naka's *nami nami* here plays on the phonetic similarity between 'wave' and the invocation's '*namu*'. Through such instances of wordplay, the arising and vanishing of all things, previously observable in 'Fautrier's Birds', is thus presented as being permeated by *busshō* ('Buddha-nature').

'Hakata' also testifies to the breadth of Naka's reading of traditional Japanese literature, as his appended notes to the opening section – translated in this collection – make clear. Among the poetic techniques Naka gathers from traditional Japanese poems themselves is the *kakekotoba*, or 'pivot-word', in which a single word can be read in two ways depending on if it is read in conjunction with what precedes or follows it. An example appears in the following lines of 'Hakata':

where are their voices now   sunk to the bottom of

the sea

waves of vexation's evening darkness rolling in rolling in

The *yū* ('evening') of *yūyami* ('evening darkness'), as Naka's note explains, puns on the homophonous *iu* ('to say'). Chikako and I have tried to indicate this elsewhere in the line through the 'say' sound embedded within 'vexation'. This reading of *yū* as *iu* means that the surrounding words could also be interpreted as 'the bottom of the sea's / darkness'. This has been attempted in the translation through creating the possibility of reading 'sea / waves' as a phrase that runs across the line break.

In his note on 'Hakata', Naka explains how the 'scenes' he saw when he returned to his hometown in 1972 'called up historical associations that clung to the places themselves': what we see and hear around us is thus conditioned by our language and culture. This feeds into his conception of words as 'things': because they are unique combinations of their visual, phonetic and 'historical' aspects, 'their translation', as he puts it in 'Notes for a Poetics', is '*fundamentally* impossible' (Naka's emphasis). In this work, he gives the onomatopoeia *shin shin* in *shin shin to yuki ga furu* ('the snow falls *shin shin*') as an example. It 'immediately calls to mind a psychological response':

> To a Japanese, it would be impossible to hear the sound *shin shin* cut off from this response. But this is something that operates within one language system, and in another language system, it would be impossible to have such a response. If an American were to lament the impossibility of its translation, our response must be that that goes without saying.

As Naka then realises, however, *shin shin* can be traced back to the Chinese *cén cén* (used to indicate precipitation) or *shēn shēn* ('deep'). A language and a culture, too, have no inherent existence: they also consist of parts assembled from other languages and cultures. The 'psychological response' to a word will also differ, even within a language system, from one person or time to another. Translation can only be deemed 'possible' if it embraces the inevitability of such change.

The use of poetic allusion in Naka's poetry is also evident in 'Passing Shower Thoughts', from his next collection, *Kūga sanbō nichijō sono ta* ('No-Self Mountain Temple Diary and Other Poems', 1985). In addition to the references to the haikai poets Matsuo Bashō (1644–1694), Yosa Buson (1716–1784), and a number of Bashō's haikai disciples, as acknowledged in Naka's own notes to the poem, the influence of the modernist poet Nishiwaki Junzaburō's famous poem 'Ame' ('Rain') is also visible. In 'Rain', a 'quiet, gentle procession of goddesses' rain down upon an unspecified town and 'soaked the sea, soaked the sand, soaked the fish. / Quietly soaked the temples, the public baths and the theatres'. Likewise, in 'Passing Shower Thoughts', the repetition of Nishiwaki's poem can be found in the rain 'quietly soaking the roots of Tenmangū Shrine's camphor trees / soaking the phantom deer and the monkeys in the zoo / washing clean the black kites' wings and the crows on withered branches'. 'Passing Shower Thoughts' thus combines traditional and modern Japanese poetic imagery.

Naka's 'Season-Word Glossary of Sounds', from his final collection *Chinkonka* ('Requiems', 1995), is a meditation upon the Japanese onomatopoeia discussed in his 'Notes for a Poetics', whose music he had already heard in the *saya saya* rustle of the sweetcorn in 'Autumn Walk'. (A 'Season-Word Glossary' – *Saijiki* – is a reference book for writers of haiku poems. Each haiku traditionally employs a season-word: particular objects or events are assigned by convention to particular seasons.) Chikako and I agree with Naka's view of the 'impossibility' of translating such onomatopoeia, and so we have left them in the original Japanese. The 'sounds' in the title are the Japanese onomatopoeia. That of 'January', for example, is *shiin*:

20

the fields, the hills and the trees are *shiin* – silent
the unfamiliar blank page   *shiin* – the soundless
illusion of sound   is it the *shin* of *shinkan*, the
forest's silence?   or the *shin* of *shinchin*, composure?
is it *shin*, the heart?   or a sign of *shin*, the morning?

The possible roots of this onomatopoeia given above – *shinkan*, *shinchin*, and both instances of *shin* that follow – are all Chinese in origin, thus again demonstrating how verbal connotations spread across languages and cultures. Moreover, it shows how even to a native speaker a word will only ever be partially known; it therefore testifies to the indeterminacy of its associations. A non-Japanese reader may form different associations; but in doing so, he or she is just another participant, like the poet, in the ever-shifting development of such associations across time and space.

Another instance of such fruitful cross-cultural influence is Naka's nō play, *Shikōtei* ('The First Emperor'), which was published in 2003 by Shichōsha and first performed at the National Noh Theatre in Tokyo on 20 March 2014, a few months before Naka passed away. Nō is a traditional Japanese form of theatre that rose to prominence in the late fourteenth and early fifteenth century with the plays of Kanami Kiyotsugu and his son, Zeami Motokiyo. Many of these reflect the dominance of the Buddhist worldview shared by Kanami, Zeami, and their patrons, the Ashikaga shōguns; but many others also praise the longevity of the emperor's rule. *Takasago*, for example, compares it to the evergreen pine, which is said to flower once every thousand years: the source for this metaphor is given as Shi Huangdi, the first emperor of China who unified the country during the short-lived Qin dynasty. *The First Emperor* examines this metaphor by depicting Shi Huangdi's quest to discover the Elixir of Life that he believed to exist on the mythical Mount Penglai across the ocean to the east. According to Sima Qian's *The Historical Records*, the principal source for Naka's play, the emperor sent the court sorcerer Xu Fu out of the Qin capital, Xianyang, with 'three thousand young boys and girls and a few hundred ships for the journey'. After setting sail, they were never heard of again.

In the second part of the play, as is common in nō, the spirits of the first part's main characters appear on stage. Whereas in the first part the First Emperor had claimed that his reign would last as long as the pine tree whose 'thousand years of jade green fill the world', the metaphor for imperial rule alluded to in *Takasago*, Xu Fu realises that 'Even the pine that lasts a thousand years will rot', and that 'at last I have come to realise / the vanity of searching for the Elixir of Life'. In the final lines, the chorus sings that the First Emperor's spirit

> mingles with the clouds of the great void,
> and turns into cosmic dust,
> and turns into cosmic dust.

Even the emperor cannot escape the principle that 'All things in the cosmos move from *mu* to *mu*'. The play also forms a fitting conclusion to Naka's own life before it, too, returned to *mu* on 1 June 2014. His life was dedicated to examining the transience of things, but also to the celebration of their beauty: though they are fleeting, the things of this world – such as the spring meltwater that 'peacefully trickles' in 'Season-Word Glossary of Sounds' – are 'filled to the brim with light'.

ANDREW HOUWEN, 13 December 2017

Translators' Note

The first thing that might strike a reader previously unacquainted with Naka's work is the near-absence of punctuation in our translation. This is in fact a common characteristic of both traditional and modern poetry in the Japanese language. We felt that it would be best to preserve this feature of the Japanese as much as possible, inserting additional punctuation only where the English makes it absolutely necessary. This can result in the creation of fruitful ambiguities like those made possible in Naka's Japanese. Where he does regularly use commas and full stops, as in 'Mist' and *The First Emperor*, we have done the same.

When written in Latin script, Japanese makes use of macrons over the vowels 'o' and 'u' ('ō' and 'ū'). These indicate that the vowel has a longer pronunciation; in traditional Japanese poetry, each instance would count as two syllables. Thus, 'nō' would count as two syllables and 'Bashō' as three. We have used these wherever they occur in Japanese, except for well-known place names such as Kyoto and Tokyo.

For information on the order of Japanese people's names, please see the note on page 8.

All notes that appear immediately after poems are Naka's; translators' notes on the poems can be found at the back of the book along with an index of Japanese authors, artists, literary works and historical figures mentioned in poems or notes.

Andrew Houwen
Chikako Nihei

from ETUDES, 1950

STREET SCENE

in the quiet street
not even the sound of footsteps on the pavement
the shutters drawn down over all the windows

where has the murmuring leaves' gold dust gone?
where has the pale-faced woman consumed by illness
staring all day from a second-floor balcony vanished?

reddish brown buildings   their doors nailed shut
now only the bones of branches piercing the chilly air

god   now there is no-one even to call your name

beyond zinc roofs the endlessly open sea
on a tower an unseen flag flutters

TREES

dull   heavy
the earth under undulating piles
of lead-coloured rubble
crushed   gasping
dark   dismal vacancy

ah   in this bitterly heavy scene
still persevering, the dusty trees!
already for so long
in the chinks of clouds not a glimmer of light
in the air not a breath of wind

emaciated naked trunks supporting
burnt-up brown diseased leaves
twisted branches bereft of birdsong

still enduring trees
existing, nothing more   on your own
how I choke when I look at you!

SHORT PIECE

caught in a net of emerald-coloured light
glimmers   shadows   the trembling green-gold illusion
of a butterfly dozing in the woods   reflected in water

in the quiet, dark green algal colloid
blinding light splintering and converging
on silver-leaf wings weaves a water lily

is glittering life a floating dream?
to the melody of a breeze rippling the water   trembling
                                                                    flowers
release their iridescent fragrances

deep inside flowery eyelids   pure sadness gleams
colourful distance palely dissolves in air   emptiness
does the sky reflect it?   a god's absence

from

ANTHOLOGY OF POST-WAR POETS, 1954

SCENE I

summer 1945

in the warmth of the rank weeds
the snakes' eggs   have they perished yet

in the distance burnt shrivelled trees
no longer
have any trace of life
only the skeletons of apartments

where the smell of the rocky shore drifts
a cavern –
time's insides
gone

the spider's web doesn't even tremble

the remains of a departed god –
under the spiral staircase's
broken spring

wildly twisted lead pipes
spout the gleaming blades
of purity's absence

SCENE II

summer 1945

scabs of black memory tear off
the guillotine river cuts up
the city's torn skin

pushed along in the flow
countless burnt eyes
eyes
eyes

in the iridescent light
the guts of civilisation crumble like broken tiles
sticking out, a rib
a malleus
a thigh bone
nerve fibres tangled around them
like rusty phone wire

where are unravelled organs
starting to sound again?

in the collapsed temple's hollowed eye-sockets
the illusion of poppies
burning silently

SCENE III

1950

under dull tin   cataract eyes
a scabies-ridden town   gone to pieces but starting to
                                              rebuild

over withered weeds   among the rubble
passing through like phantoms   egg-coloured
                                              peach-coloured cars

chimneys sticking their necks out of dented roofs
emit the smoke of miserable routine
leaning on the rusty railing of distrust   I smoke cheap
                                              Golden Bat

the root and purpose of existence   out of sight already
                                              long ago
or rather   after discovering their infinite absence –

silently like clouds   grey cats wander the sky's canopy
endlessly expanding rootless world   life without direction

and why must the flayed rocky shore echo with nightmares
o absent gods

torn rags hung down from the sky
distantly from the northwest   a foaming tide of curses
                                              and suffering echoes

the future approaching everyone
floating there   something resembling a rat's corpse

LANDSCAPE WITH FISHBONES

climbing up a glass spiral staircase
a decrepit monstrous beast   all its hair gone
the only one remaining   a desert stretches
in front of the blind being's eyes
here and there huge things like fishbones protrude
drawing the eye like a paper kite   the desiccated
                                        image of a god

in the clear ether of the sky
hira hira hira hira
endlessly fluttering down like banknotes
like millions of pages   torn to pieces
the sublimated anguish and the cries
of a people that had destroyed itself
by the well into which they sank
not even a dream of the world's beginning
nor even a shadow of reincarnation remain

in the far distance
a half-transparent sun like a broken watch
half-buried in the sand

in the skull   dark womb covered in wrinkles   through
intercourse with what god   was it born   twitching
spasmodically   the eerie foetus does not let him sleep
now and again it stomps strangely   writhing to reach the
brightness outside – yet between the tongue and the teeth   or
between the index and the middle finger   gleaming brightly
on the white page   perhaps no more than a dead tapeworm

smouldering in the ashtray   the vain fragrant smoke of
time   in the study a gloomy altar lined with grave markers
like ammunition in a magazine   buried in the coffins smelling
of silver fish   the remains of thoughts   were one lid to open
then from within the stiffened ugly corpse   countless black
fingertips   would reach out seeking to be reborn   writhing
maggots   tapeworms like long-necked monsters   people's
discarded worldly desires once   linger in eye-sockets   eat
into intestinal walls   and crawl into others' bodies   this
deep craving   is the ancestral curse of the karma   of people
imitating their creator   even now squirming in its perverted
womb   the same worldly desires

sleepless fearful fireflies burning with their own light   the
porcelain dish of frozen time   the awakening images within
images   in its silence

as soon as he had passed through the landscape of the thin
paper sheet   and twisted his body to peer through it from
underneath   something spilled out from his insides   on the
noon asphalt   like a thread of smoke, a silence rose from the
bustle   then   his feet floated just two inches off the ground
he quickly tried to bring his feet down again   but his feet
would just keep swimming in space   no matter what he did
the two-inch gap between his soles and the ground   just
would not return to how it had been   the silence that had
threaded its way through the bustle   became a transparent
sea overhead   silently expanding without limit

the next day and the day after   passing through broken
walls   through the bodies of cars   through the gaps in
rows of bone-like trees   through the tawdry camouflage of
streets   he walked   but though he walked and walked he
could not make the space between his soles and the ground
disappear   the edge of the landscape of the thin paper sheet
kept receding   no matter what he did   he couldn't enter
the landscape   and the pale sea sank down from above   like
noctilucae, electronic signs   like gauze obstruct the eyes
that would peer through this world from underneath

from then on year after year   time was like air   he still
passed through the landscape, peering through it from
underneath   despairingly he screamed 'o mother earth!'
reaching for the ground   but when he approached the two
inches' distance   the earth would still remain two inches
away   like appearances and their shadows never merging,
forever in vain   no matter what, he would not stay on the
ground

from ANTHOLOGY OF CONTEMPORARY
POETS, 1959

DÉCALCOMANIE II

shi (poem)   is a needle's gleam spreading on the marble
me (eye)   is the magnet on which its light converges

shi (death)   is invisible sap climbing inside a tree
me (bud)   is the thorn it feeds pricking the outside world

*

shi (poem)   is the shadow of a soaring bird
me (eye)   is the rifle bullet following in its tracks

shi (death)   is a moth's disturbance circling the night's crown
me (bud)   is the flame subsiding on the candlestick

*

shi (poem)   is a black rose
me (eye)   is the trembling antenna

shi (death)   is the sea-bed's tangled algae
me (bud)   is the slicing blade

*

shi and *shi*   are the ciphers
me and *me*   are the decipherers

shi and *shi*   are the pollen
me and *me*   are the carriers

POEM I

pale consciousness drops
saliva onto a white page
trembling like the silhouette
of a distantly echoing fountain
like the pistil of a narcissus
it no longer
has any ethical purpose
any aesthetic aim
the sticky touch
of its life is the tragic
light shining
in the false window
of its yellow existence
a poem to pass the time
to endure simply existing
its emptiness
is the gleam of yesterday's rain
on the worm's back drying on the sand
or
washing onto the shore, the jellyfish's w   h   i   s   p   e   r

the feeling of lying down
with white moss
growing on your tongue
and a cold stomach
calls to mind an epitaph
packed rows of letters
close their eyelids
fragile as stones
as logic breaks down
pale blue smoke rises
as from a lemon
a twelve-tone piece rises
in the waves
of distant youthful days
of memories buried in the sand
like quietly burning violets
jellyfish
human spirits drifting up from a thicket of words
or rather
pale sorrow

bread! you say and bread exists
stone! you say and a stone exists
thus words, like existence, have a tremendous power
through these withered leaves
where does this white road lead?
while biting into bread and kicking a stone
black thoughts swirl around the mind like whips
in a dragonfly's trembling transparent wings
the tone of a violin gleams
but what exists here is the word stone
not the physical stone
the word stone is another, separate thing
from the physical stone
it is not just that a white horse is not a horse
it is that a horse is already not a horse
turning its head towards the depths of autumn
what is it that the horse is thinking?
an empty car stranded on a ridge
is like the vast compound eyes of the dragonfly
those vast compound eyes watch the green horizon
the green horizon contains infinite life
there a farmer like a philosopher pulls up radishes
thus from outward and inward things
a poet skilfully pulls up fine words like radishes
and so words infinitely modulate
in the organic connections of their world
sweetcorn withers by the roadside
like the image of a transparent thing
or like a wind-blown woman in an Ebihara Kinosuke painting
withered leaves of the sweetcorn rustle, *saya saya*
its music is deeper than autumn
a painting is more existence-like than existence

but music goes beyond it towards infinity
thus the transparent sky is filled with music
scattering withered leaves and leaves of speech
all life vanishes in that direction

I hurried. Dreadful mist everywhere. The road twisted and turned through the foul mist smelling like strange offal, heading towards its dark insides. No idea where I was going. I just had to hurry. Like a man drowning in music, my flesh faded away, my anxious mind swam in space. I had to go somewhere. I'm hurrying. But what I crawled into was that shabby room. In front of the wall, a familiar man laughs. Yes, I recognize him. But for some reason I couldn't remember the guy's name.

– Is this mist? No. It's your vacant mind. For twenty years you've wandered about, smoking thirty cigarettes a day. So up to now your lungs have breathed out emptiness two hundred and nineteen thousand times. These hanging mist-clouds are your past. It stinks. What have you been doing for twenty years? You narrowly escaped death, you survived the war. For the sake of stupidity, you fell in love. For the sake of bread, you lost hair and wore out the soles of your shoes. And from time to time you wiped words like bloody phlegm on bits of tissue paper. But you haven't changed a bit. Still vacant. If anything, then ultimately nothing. Hardly a great epitaph. You're a moth trapped in a cocoon of smoke. Your words just trace the cocoon's inside. You can never reach 'meaning' or 'experience'. Why see everything only from the perspective of nothingness? – Don't be so anxious, you're not going anywhere. Hey, are you smoking again? Fine, in any case the only thing I can say is that after your four-hundred-thousandth breath you'll completely vanish. Ha ha.

I blew tobacco smoke fiercely into his sneering face. Like a hundred years rising out of Urashima's box, the cords of smoke wound into his nostrils and, in an instant, there was dreadful mist everywhere.

from Music, 1965

Mu is not 'nothing'. It is the *mu* of existing things, breathing *mu*, the *mu* of writhing waves. It is because music sounds in these things, or perhaps in order to make music sound, that people produce words. Just as the world's essence is *mu*, to create words is related to the essence of life. What is created achieves an independence from what created it. Through the action of creating, the creating subject is cut loose from what it has created. It allows this creation to exist on its own. It is itself always returned to *mu*. I do not know whether words express *mu* or conceal it. In any case, because words are created through the process of *mu*, they are not the possession of any particular individual. They do not belong to the present, nor are they merely the progeny of what are barely three generations of modern poetry; they are created on the basis of the life and function of well over a thousand years of the Japanese language. Aiming for what is beyond manifestation, they are a drop of *sake* poured into a limitless ocean, a small offering to the even vaster *mu*.

Fautrier   four *tori e*   four birds painting
one bird purple
one bird green
two birds transparent
skim through a magnetic storm
perturbed purple
gathered green
scud through the gouache   sharply
steel skygleam before dawn spills through the windowframe
cold clawmarks'
unseen tracks
unheard ether of flutes
sky done in clay
clouds of waves
waves
waves
waves
purple the burning flame of *mu*
green the predawn bud-sap
the birds fly through the invisible shadows of birdless forms
whirling world
turning time
the birds forever flying
never arriving
never stopping
at themselves
solid wind
whirlpool poem
large looming music
endlessly emerging from themselves

the birds do not stop flying
the whip of purple's *mu*
the predawn green's
wake...

po

poe

poetry

yyyyyyy...

smouldering waves of pipe smoke
trembling spots on gently sunlit
slender jade wings of sleep
invisible time-flow's mist-patterns
invisible birds in misty tree-tops
invisible leaves of trees
invisible leaves of speech
invisible fog
of the mind's memories
distant turquoise of tearful eyes
far away on a floating bridge
in darkening air sorrowful forms misting over
silently longing
solemnly streaming
pale smoke of the breath of people's lives
skimming intertwined ivy's trembling leaves
the pale barefoot anxious steps
of drooping branches' cold drops
a fleeting glimpse of fragrant amber's
iridescence in tangled clouds of tears
waves of illusory lulling algal shadows
like fins flapping like folds of skirts
the patterned grain of the dark pipe's thick smell of tar

AFTER A PAINTING

when I woke up it was noon
because the wall clock is a faceless ghost
and the room is completely still
as if photographed at a high shutter speed   I gradually
                                                          get up
a painter friend then comes in
'a present for you'
a pale apparition caught on the threshold's frame

the crucified   apparition of a woman
a green snake twined around her breasts
though the white starfish lily's fragrance rises
the dark pupils   of the woman blind to all the fires of life
distantly stare in a different direction
as if it were the mind's eternal absence
or eternal *mu* that she were looking at

'it's a portrait of your lover
if you add odd numbers together you might get an even one'
the friend laughed voicelessly
pale woman
at the heart of noon's faceless dialless clock
that's why I slept with you   so my exterior
could shape your empty interior

floating in the pupils reflecting *mu*
your tears are transparent cherries
frozen fruit of the future
when torn apart and caught on the tip of the tongue
split in two   cold bitterness
runs along the harp-strings of my ribs
sharper than death life's trembling melody pierces me

SHI (DEATH) OR *SHI* (POETRY)

when I go to meet you
you are always   not there
in the shadows of the lace curtains
in the dark stains of the walls
in the drifting smoke
of the stubbed cigarette on the table
not there
only the ashtray's desert   silently
dispersing time's white bones
invisible thorns pierce
the back of the dark red throat's
fleeing birds
I keep walking for no reason
suddenly from behind
for no reason   you cover my eyes with your hands
when I turn around
only the dazzling blue, blue sky
you are already
out of reach
shimmering like sunlight
in the memory of an amnesiac

now   you are a stranger
but once
you were a kind friend's face   never to return again
and once
you were my real mother's face   that I have never seen
stirring the water's surface
the pouring rain of the piano strings
soaked in the pale music
it is always you
who come to meet me

SEA

the glitter of a thousand scattered cicada wings

someone
swimming out to the offing
a rock

endless waves waves waves waves waves
swelling rising flooding breaking precipitous
the foam of *mu*
the sand's skin absorbs the seed of emptiness
its eternal piano performance
of rippling light

black wood
illusory seat
under the lascivious algal tangle
of a languid morning's smell of coffee
the fossilised
pale shell
of a woman's pale behind

octopus   a burst of laughter
disappointment

the gleam of death by a thousand piercing bee-stings

eternally unreturning
summer

trees   are fireworks that spring from the earth's life   the floral
wreaths of a giant dragonfly opening its wings in mid-air   the
bursting of a thousand sparkling threads   though they may
seem like a time-stopped fossil   they're in a different time
dimension where ten years are a second   ceaselessly changing
to bud-green, beige, maroon   between those branches my
grandfathers vanished…   among these bursting branches
too my father will vanish   launched fireworks try to grasp
the void   burning up in a thousand transient years

in a flash from the head a slim white trunk catches fire, is
suddenly licked by the tongue of a blue-red-purple flame,
turns into electrified Nichrome wire, and in an instant the
cast-off shell of lace thread collapses   the transient burning
of a single match   the last flash of the ground's long-faded
firework   reincarnated in a distant phase   now   in
the tumbling tangle of smouldering pipe-smoke   I watch
playing back a thousand years in vain   a slow-motion video
of strange life's illusion

SHORT PIECE

when the sakura pickle sent by a female friend
from Suma floats in boiling water
the unseasonal petals open
like a silk negligée, sakura-coloured,
the salty taste on the tip of the tongue
like the fragrance of a woman's v
and the blue, blue sky dazzling the eyes
are like a Mozart melody
in a battlefield's deathly silence
in unreturning time's distant illusory sound
of thoughts of the life refused and left behind
by the boy running endlessly over the sand
like the voice of the wind in the pines
waves swell, approach, and return
tears are the pearl drops of passing showers
the tangled sheets' pale naked apparition
is reflected in the floating petals' water

PALM LANDSCAPE

on the hill where no grass-blade grows or moves like a strange
                                        living thing
thoughts of the road on which comings and goings endlessly
                                        cross and separate
rise like the flames of diving women's seaweed burned to
                                        extract the salt
all the roads persistently head to a distant unseen end
over pink flesh   and the groundwater of pale blood
darkly cut like the see-through veins of withered leaves
each fatal line wavers, tangles, breaks off and intertwines
where will each approach and recede from the other?
quietly slowly growing old alone in the dry sand
as the shapes of countless sorrowful rivers stream in parallel,
are buried in ripples of swirling sand and, finally, at the
                                        cape's edge,
freeze with fear   they are struck by the wind of thirst's
                                        murderous whip
grasping at *mu*   the trembling of the fingers
gripping the cliff-edge

from HAKATA, 1975

waves

      waves waves

            waves waves waves waves

dark waves destructive waves disintegrating waves

swelling waves seething waves spent waves

      breaking

      smashing

      splintering

      falling

tearing waves'   buds of tears

namu namu Amida Buddha   buddha buddha beating beating

streaming seaweed's murmur of memories

      vanished in the foam

      floating in the heart of the deep-sea whirlpool

      the bell cape's evening voice

waves of heavy thoughts   waves of heavy ships

longing for what   plaintive voices in Ōshima Bay

where are their voices now   sunk to the bottom of the sea

waves of vexation's evening darkness rolling in rolling in

these white lines are ripples of foam

expended bubbles   the Wa land of Na's

Umi no Nakamichi shore forming a cogon-grass ring

beyond the wavering algae of Kashiigata   Hakozaki beach

remotest regions'   the capital's   Sumiyoshi's   Suminoe's

      Sokotsutsu-no-o

      Nakatsutsu-no-o

      Uwatsutsu-no-o

asking the sacred fence's pine the way in leaves of speech

to the sky between the stones of Pine Moon Hut's

                        Dewdrop Well

two rats   racing against one another

four snakes   fighting to get ahead

as birds fly across the scene   towards the dark red dawn

and out of the gap a white horse gallops   towards the
                                              gleaming dusk
in the endlessly unravelling threads of time
the pale-ink Sode Harbour turns into the town of seven
                                                    streams
the illusions spun by the crab-spider's claws
are the colour of rain falling on the same world's leaves of pine
after melancholy autumn's
distant blood-coloured clouds scatter
        people's lives in this land of Tsukushi

Each word that structures a poetic work is always open to a multitude of possible interpretations; each reader may construct their own meaning in response to their own perceptions. While it goes without saying that neither the intention of the poet himself nor the process of the work's composition have any privilege over the reader's freedom, nevertheless, by giving notes, the writer can sometimes be tempted to guide the reader in a particular direction. Discussing one's own work is no more than a kind of self-concealment. It is not uncommon for the true meanings of the work to remain unconsciously hidden. For the reader, too, such notes might be unwanted and unnecessary, and might be felt to restrict the freedom of their imagination all the more; nevertheless, I have attempted these notes while taking this into account.

'Hakata' was written in the autumn of 1972. What spurred the composition of the poem was my return after an interval of many years to Hakata, where I was born, in the summer of the year before. I returned once more in the summer of 1972. I walked around here and there in the streets of the town where I spent my childhood, which had completely changed since then. I visited Dazaifu Shrine, Kannon Temple and Kaidanin Temple, and also crossed over to Shika Island. The scenes my eyes saw always seemed to be illusions – that is, together with my own memories of my childhood, they called up historical associations that clung to the places themselves, enticing me to compose poetic words suggested by the interlayered substances of the world around me. For me, the meaning of composing a poem, it goes without saying, is not simply the individual expression of emotion, but rather, perhaps, what kind of general word-structure, or what kind of music the string of 'a'-vowels in 'Hakata' can create.

'Hakata I' is guided by the autonomous movement of the word *nami* (wave) and aims to show the gradual approach of the absent 'Hakata'. This word, which suggests the image of the sea, at the same time indicates the word 無み (*nami*, 'nought' or 'to set at nought'). The journey towards the annihilated 'Hakata' is conducted by the decorative linked-verse patterns of traditional poetry. Of course, the poem's particular historical climate suggests the method. It is the writer's intention to conceal his thoughts in it. Even if no knowledge of such sources is applied, the rhythm can thus move the reader.

(Regarding the opening's *nami / nami nami / nami*, Sakaguchi Hiroshi's 'The Structure of Naka Tarō's "Hakata"' (*Kuragō*, no. 23) interprets *naminami* as also being able to mean *na minami*. *Na* could then be read as 汝 or 奴 (那). In the case of the former, 汝 can be used as a first- or second-person pronoun, and *minami* ('south') can simply mean 'southwards' when looking at Hakata from the direction of Tokyo. The latter can be the *na* (奴) in the so-called Seal of the Na King of Wa (a gold seal given by the Chinese Emperor Guangwu to an envoy from Na, a Western part of Wa, Japan, in the first century CE), or the *na* of 那津 (Nanotsu, 'Na Harbour'), an old name for Hakata. In any case, his interpretation suggested that it is perhaps more appropriate to read *naminaminaminami* as *na minami na minami* ('me/you southwards me/you southwards', or 'Na southwards Na southwards') than *nami nami nami nami* ('waves waves waves waves').)

breaking / smashing / splintering / falling: from Minamoto no Sanetomo in his *Collection of the Kamakura Minister*, 'The vast sea's roaring waves, breaking, smashing, splintering, falling onto the rocks'.

vanished in the foam / floating in the heart of the deep-sea whirlpool / the bell cape's evening voice: by Shōtetsu in the tenth volume of his *Collection of Grass Roots*. This *uta* ('song') is itself based on the following preceding works:

From the seventh volume of the *Manyōshū* ('Collection of Ten Thousand Leaves'), 'Though we have passed beyond the raging sea of the bell cape, we have not forgotten the gods of Shika Island'.

From the seventeenth volume of the *Kokinshū* ('Collection of the Past and Present'), 'Nothing remains of what vanished in the foam rolling in with the sea's tide' (author unknown).

From the eighteenth volume of the *Shinkokinshū* ('New Collection of the Past and Present'), by Fujiwara no Ietaka, 'Waka bay – floating in with the sea's tide, tell me who despairs where my loved ones are'.

From the tenth volume of the *Shinshokukokinshū* ('New Collection of the Past and Present Continued'), by Shiga Yoshishige, 'The sound coming from the bell cape while sleeping on a sea voyage – dreams also go with the waves into the distant night'.

longing for what   plaintive voices of Ōshima Bay: from the 'Tamakazura' chapter of *The Tale of Genji*, 'Who is it the sailors long for? Listening to plaintive voices in Ōshima Bay'.

where are their voices now   sunk to the bottom of the sea: from Bashō, 'Where is the moon now? The bell has sunk to the bottom of the sea'. Bashō's hokku refers to the 'bell cape' at Tsuruga, but the fishermen of Tsuruga's 'bell cape' are said originally to have come from the 'bell cape' of Chikuzen.

waves of vexation's evening darkness: there is a pivot word (*kakekotoba*) here: the *yū* ('evening') of *yūyami* ('evening darkness') puns on the homophonous *iu* ('to say').

rolling in rolling in / these white lines are ripples of foam: from Hagiwara Sakutarō's poem 'Spring Night' in his collection *Howling at the Moon*, 'Rolling in, rolling in, / these white lines of waves are ripples'.

Umi no Nakamichi forming a cogon-grass ring: from Sōgi's *Journey Along the Tsukushi Road*, 'Umi no Nakamichi's path was really like a cogon-grass ring'.

beyond the floating algae of Kashiigata   Hakozaki beach: from the sixth volume of the *Manyōshū*, by Ono no Oyu. Among others, his *uta,* 'The time of the winds has come – in Kashiigata Bay where the tide has gone out, let us go and harvest the algae'.

remotest regions'   the capital's   Sumiyoshi's: in the *Records of the Origins of Sumiyoshi Shrine*, this *uta* is ascribed to Shōtetsu: 'Both remotest regions and the capital are good places to live – Sumiyoshi Village'. It is doubtful that such a poor *uta* could have been written by Shōtetsu, but even now it is commemorated as such along the right-hand path in the grounds of Sumiyoshi Shrine.

Sokotsutsu-no-o / Nakatsutsu-no-o / Uwatsutsu-no-o: the three gods worshipped at Sumiyoshi Shrine.

asking the sacred fence's pine the way in leaves of speech: from Sōgi, *Journey Along the Tsukushi Road*, based on the legend of the pine that grew in one night: 'I will ask the pine of the sacred fence in leaves of speech, will I soon find the right way again?'

to the sky between the stones of Pine Moon Hut's Dewdrop Well: from the *Records of the Origins of Sumiyoshi Shrine*: 'A scribe at the temple of Tōfukuji, the Zen master Shōtetsu, who loved beautiful views, built the Pine Moon Hut and created the Dewdrop Well beside the shrine, where he enjoyed the refinement of tea ceremony.' The remains of these can still be seen. There is no historical record that Shōtetsu moved there, so it is difficult to believe this account. It is thought that the coincidence between one of his other names, Shōgetsuan ('Pine Moon Hut'), and that of the hut is the origin of this legend.

two rats racing against one another: from the fifth volume of the *Manyōshū*, in Yamanoue no Okura's introduction to 'Japanese Elegies', 'Two rats race against one another, four snakes fight to get ahead – birds fly across the scene towards the dawn, a horse gallops out of the gap towards the evening'.

in the endlessly unravelling threads of time: from the *The Tales of Ise*, 'Threads spun on a spool long ago – if only we could wind back now to then'.

the pale-ink Sode Harbour: 'Sode no Minato' (lit. 'Sleeves Harbour') is an old name for Hakata. It is said to have been named as such by Taira no Kiyomori. Later, this town was repeatedly ravaged by war, but it was revived by Toyotomi Hideyoshi.

the illusions spun by the crab-spider's claws: from Shōtetsu's *Collection of Grass Roots*, 'Things Past are Like a Dream'. 'Spun by the crab-spider's claws, this world is the floating bridge of a distant thread'.

the colour of rain falling on the same world's leaves of pine: from Sōgi's *Journey Along the Tsukushi Road*, 'On the leaves of pine, the rain falls in the same world'.

melancholy autumn's: from the fourth volume of the *Kokinshū* (author unknown), 'Watching the shadows of moonlight leaking through the trees – melancholy autumn'. From *The Tale of Genji*'s 'Suma' chapter, 'At Suma, melancholy autumn winds were blowing'.

distant blood-coloured clouds scattering: from the fifth volume of the *Manyōshū*, 'Ply over ply of white clouds scattering in the land of Tsukushi'.

the woman's long hair is a wave of streaming willow
it flows like the ripple of sorrow's river
soon turning into the slender smoke of *susuki* grass...

autumn's a bright morning shore's struggling fish
turning into a withered tree's shadow
transparent like a cicada husk's or an ant-lion's wings...

the autumn woman's skin has a trembling lily's scent
walking through withered leaves in the distance   time's
                                     footfall
the thirst for the far shore of the futureless blue sky...

NOVEMBER WORDS

after a thousand   scattering   folding fans'
gold   memories   flutter down
in the pale ink light   words
have the sadness of dried withered leaves

as the scattered showers mournfully
skim the evening woods
the clear ears   of cold stones
listen to the spluttering of time

when night falls   words
like shadows intertwined in withered ivy
expand the net within us

and so   deep in the night
floating in the dull muddy water
they become   an illusion of lotus-flowers

MEMORY

reeling sea
whirling whirlpool
avalanching   rolling   columbines of waves'
time   endlessly unravels and dissolves   a rope,
                                                                a bubble
the dark tangle of streaming sargassum's
grainy memories   fades into the distance
in the crack of refracted jade light
seabirds' cries
blood-cut clouds
stone sky of the blinded city
death's   phantom soldiers

OPUS*

the season of mists streaming away
turns from gold and silver to pale black
revolving magic lanterns return once more
distant sun scatters, the light of cicada wings scatters
everything turns from today to yesterday, from yesterday to
tomorrow
the visible turns into the invisible
what is turns into what is not
time turns into the feet of rain running along the strings of
harps
the white flame of a thousand-year candle burns
in the lake   of cataract eyes shaded by the lashes
of the empty heart's tangled canopy
weaving patterns of scattered showers' spray
mingle with dimly brightening ripples of memory
winter's glittering fireflies   summer's frost-needles in the
dawn
spring's white bones of waving *susuki* grass beginning to wither
in the floating thought of the naked fragrance
like clear water
of your yellow-green and light-green light kimono
the illusion of wavering curves of thighs and calves
allows the burning tangled algal hair to cling
now floating, now sinking   in the dazzling dissolving light
of endless waves of wavering dreams
the neither passing nor not passing of the pierced heart
its neither going nor not going is the light of long ago
on the transparent gleaming waterfowl wings
of time's birds
flying into the emptiness of the sky

OPUS**

omnia mutantur, nihil interit

falling falling flickering rain's
pale acetylene flame becomes
fireflies bursting from the dark
wavy hair of drowsy wavering
gleaming in the pools of grass
because there is no birth or death
they pass away in stony fields
the flicker in a hart's eyes
eventually ripens into an olive
reviving in a clear dawn's coffin
as time neither passes nor doesn't
pass the distant beat of egrets'
wings in the pale algal streaming
clouds like the rising fragrance
of rainbows in the phantom sky
while mutating without end
in the endlessly quivering heart's
eternal song calls the reply
of the spirit of words echoing
in a space without dimension

OPUS***

shivering winter's sunlit stepping stones crumble
unseen time's distant green thorns and mosses crumble
reddened, stems of ferns and grapevines dissolve
jujube dates and sacred bamboo also soundlessly wither
the dark flame spun in a whirlpool of dazzling light
silently burning up and falling to pieces   the gleam of ash

*

Marianne's phantom voice crosses
the path of memory's echoing garden and yesterday's trees
crossing the cloister of entwined ferns' and grapevines' patterns
from the dark depths of the mirror of time's closed door
a shadow's flicker darkens in a leaning shoulder's hollow
oh   summer's streaming blonde hair   glossy silk
the cicada husks' thin sorrowful wings
beaten by the pale violent waves of a passing shower's spray
filled with the wavering dreams of lilies' scent
from the marble-smooth morning's pillowed flesh
brimming honey the tremble of the ripe wild bunches of grapes
the tilted windpipe's tremble is a flame rising into the sky
turning into ripples lapping the waterside's green scum
the apricot dawn's echoing phantom voice

*

in the flowing water's gleam the ice's music sparkles
time's towers rise in waves of clouds forming jellyfish
in the tongues of tangling twining rising flames
the melody of the rosemallow's pale death trembles
the brush's path turns back on itself, the wind calms, the sand
                                  disappears
the eternally burning fire guarding the picture scroll subsides

73

from NO-SELF MOUNTAIN TEMPLE DIARY
AND OTHER POEMS, 1985

PASSING SUMMER

in the morning hair of a palely brightening

dawn garden's tangled grassy darkness

waves of summer's tears overflow

gone the dream of trembling lily skin

gone the white death of gardenias' scent

in first light over fields of darkness

the voice of dissolving time's distant storm

scatters revolving green's dazzling illusion

into empty sky...

OLD-STYLE OLD POND SONNET

the trees of memory sadly cross their heavy arms
in the sky's streaming silk sleeves of mourning
above the tangled algal hair   below the green water's
                              surface
wavering shadows of crosses accumulate

'the twitter of birds in the tree-tops is far away
the sun shines   the suffering of the walnut mind is dark'
the noon illusion of the twenty-year-old you
sitting on a cold stone seat watching the struggle of withered
                              leaves

... now the sunlight's a slanting stream of blood
pebbles and bones of branches dispersed in dull muddy water
the languid echo of a motorboat dredging the piles of leaves

countless glittering ripples of eyes
unsettle the far shore's silent melody
and shatter time's black leaning tower...

the season ages   gracefully
day by day as it bluely quietens
sunlight on tree roots

and time's an invisible fire climbing tree tubes
in sky expanding between the mesh of branches
in order to ripen the mellow fruit

the ageing season   one night, quietly
lets out a silver dream and departs
keeping the fruit flesh's remaining fragrance

SPRING PIGEON

for the first time in thirty-eight years   within the grounds
                                  of Nezu Gongen Shrine
from the sky in the mirror of distant days a flutter of wings, a
                                          pigeon lands
it was during the war   from the top of Hakusan for no
                                                reason
I once strolled down Dango Slope with you
to this place on that distant blue morning
if the pigeon   could be conscious of what was needed to live
it would destroy itself with fear
but three hundred and thirty-three thousand three hundred
                                      hours having passed
bathing in the arrows of soft spring light   *kururu kururu*
the pigeon still busily pecks at its feed

PASSING SHOWER THOUGHTS

a passing shower solemnly
comes creeping up on tiptoe
from beyond the distant zinc roofs of time
over the unseen iron bones and mountains of rubble
of a midwinter sunset town
soaking the bran buns and dog guts of a black market's muddy
street
soaking a long line of protesters demanding their year-end
allowances
the passing shower has turned into the pale sound of footsteps
emerging from the shabby black and white screen
of a forgotten suburban cinema
quietly soaking the roots of Tenmangū Shrine's camphor trees
soaking the phantom deer and the monkeys in the zoo
washing clean the black kites' wings and the crows on withered
branches
wetting the workshops' lit-up windows
and their piled logs and iron
striking the icy walls of high-rise buildings
with countless punctuation marks
skimming the bare bones of plane-tree rows
making the neon shopping streets glitter...
(people running like shadows
on the Setagaya Bridge)
while making the lingering evening's thousands of votive lights'
pale flames spray on the river's surface   aimlessly
the passing shower scuttles past
beyond rat-coloured time

zinc-roofed capital – Anzai Hitoshi
the passing shower quietly soaking the roots of the camphor trees –
    Buson

81

the apparitions of the deer are just the rain quickly passing by – Katō
 Shūichi
*first passing shower – the monkeys also wish for a small straw
 raincoat* – Bashō
first passing shower – also washing clean the wings of the black kites
 – Kyorai
shower passing by – lit-up windows of a home with gathered log piles
 – Bonchō
people running past on the Seta bridge fleeing the passing shower –
 Jōsō

ROMANESQUE

there is not much time left
everything is up in the air
nothing to be done   anything goes
Albrecht van der Qualen
arriving at an unknown station on an evening thick with fog
in an unknown town's   wet gas-lit street
passing through an old twin-towered gate
crossing an iron bridge over a river splitting into three
always turning left wherever he went
Albrecht van der Qualen
suddenly he reached the end of the town and then
rang the bell of a door with a *rooms to let* sign and then
what happened every night in those rented rooms?
conversation with nightmares?   a game of chess with the
                                                                              dead?
making love with alluring naked crying women?
Albrecht van der Qualen
under the silently dancing candle-flame
there is not much time left
everything is up in the air

Albrecht van der Qualen is a character in a work by Thomas Mann.

FLYING SHADOWS

what are these shadows
in rose light shining
through cracks in the pale dreams
of darkening indigo clouds?
heading southwards over wave after wave
whirling   whirling
turning   turning
screaming at the deaf sky
what are these spirits
turning   turning   turning madly
speeding through time's changing colours
the heart's tangled clouds
moving beyond the waves in thinning light
southwards southwards

from REQUIEMS, 1995

Dream • Memory

trembling lilies
quivering evening
dream's scented lily-
white fingers   coolly
gliding   gliding   over your abdomen
like sweetfish
emerging from a Delvaux painting
large-eyed
a nude waxwork woman's
pale   delinquent fingers
slowly   crawling
tickle   the skin   of your lower abdomen
(the strangeness of what's there!)
fingering the nest   of bunched grass
the suffocating scent of the quivering dream's lilies
your little bird   begins to move
(the terror of what you're feeling!)
trembling   swelling   raising its head
turning into   a water buffalo's horns

is your dream   a distant memory's   lingering echo?

December 1937, you were fifteen, and were taken to Kyūshū
University Hospital's Akaiwa Wing for an appendectomy. The
day before the operation, surrounded by the white hospital
room's white curtains, a large-eyed nurse lightly took your penis
(the strangeness of what's there!) and shaved the surrounding
pubic hair with a razor. You stared at an unmoving thin-winged
ant-lion on the white ceiling, but though you tried to keep calm
you couldn't (the terror of what you're feeling!), and your penis
slowly swelled and started rising...

That large-eyed nurse has probably already become a white-haired old woman, and is perhaps no longer of this world. Incidentally, the surgeon for that operation, a quiet, intellectual man, became involved towards the end of the war, in May 1945, in the American army prisoner of war human experimentation incident. Though he refused to take part in the experiments on American soldiers, on 27 August 1948 he was sentenced to death by hanging. However, afterwards the sentence was lightened on appeal, and on 20 January 1949 he was released. He is now eighty-four years old, living in Fukuoka city in good health.

JULY

1

the Kannon temple bell distantly echoes
the burning of the chaff   scorches the night sky of memory
fetching purifying sand   at Gion Yamakasa festival

2

the rain's harp sweeps past *allegro*
irises   peonies   rhododendrons too   swept past
from a green wound a drop drips *andante*

3

rotting grass gives birth to fireflies
a lily morphs into a butterfly
in the sky swim countless silver fish

4

one morning white waves come crashing into the mind
the endless traveller   alone
walks through beautiful southern streets

5

amid the rubble water bursts from pipes
tears are burnt and parched
darkly bright   noon

6

the author of 'Spinning Gears' drank Veronal
on an innocent young day   for the first time
I felt the terror of life

an unseen waterwheel faintly sounds in the distance
along a road smelling of daphnes
to the right   Inokashira Road
a wayside marker carved in 1722
(exactly two hundred years before I was born)
turning left I saw Taigyo ahead of me
in the distance
as I tried to call him
I realised, swallowing my words
that he was no longer someone of this world
passing through the gate, I meet someone from the past – autumn

evening

six years earlier, 1716, on this same wayside marker
a hokku by the haikai master born in Kema village
now it is not autumn but late spring
this 'someone from the past'   was this an old acquaintance
or someone no longer of this world?
– in any case they all
pass beyond this world
those I know have departed one after another,
Gyogyo, in Taigyo's renga group,
quickly passed away the same November
vanishing from this world, where did they go?
becoming distant space dust in the sky
an unseen waterwheel   the smell of daphnes
or perhaps now walking along beside me
passing through the gate, I too am a passer-by –
that eighteenth-century haikai master wrote
but he too

Taigyo is the haiku name of Sasaki Kiichi, and Gyogyo that of Noda Shinkichi. Both passed away in 1993.

SEASON-WORD GLOSSARY OF SOUNDS

JANUARY   *shiin*

like a stone's prayer   the fields, hills and trees are *shiin* –
silent   the unfamiliar blank page   *shiin* – the soundless
illusion of sound   is it the *shin* of *shinkan*, the forest's
silence?   or the *shin* of *shinchin*, composure?   is it *shin*,
the heart?   or a sign of *shin*, the morning?   soon from
under the skin of the pure white field   the earth's pulse
begins to sound

FEBRUARY   *pishiri*

suddenly the ice's colossal mirror cracks   *pishiri*   is it
the cut from a pebble thrown by something   at dawn in
Kisaragi, the second month?   is it the sickle-nails of dust
devils?   *pishiri* – in the cold air's cutting *ks*   the sound
is the sign of the coming season

MARCH   *tō tō*

meltwater gathers   the valley streams start flowing with a
tinkling *tō tō* sound   along the streams fresh grass begins to
sprout, horsetail starts to grow   *tō tō* the water peacefully
trickles, *tō tō*   filled to the brim with light   when it
reaches the fields, it still goes gently   *tapu tapu*   soaking
the grass on the banks

APRIL   *hira hira*

lightly *hira hira*   white notes and flares overlap   *hira*
hira hira hira   over the fields, over the hills, the apparition
of a butterfly flits by   *hira hira,* the tears of peach-coloured

petals dance and scatter   *hira hira hira hira*   gentle
breeze   the hum of spring

MAY   *sawa sawa*

the wind crosses, *sawa sawa*, through the trees' new
green   the spring wheat rustles, *sawa sawa*   the
trees' foliage thickens, the ears of wheat ripen into
gold   murmuring *zawa zawa,* and yet   a moment
ago still *sawa sawa,* serene   *sawayaka*, fresh, is an autumn
season-word   and yet the fifth month too   is *sawayaka*

JUNE   *shito shito*

shito shito shito shito shito shito shito shito   Musashino's snowbell
blossoms   Tsukushi's soapberry blossoms   Ogasawara's
wiliwili blossoms   Kisakata's silktree blossoms   drooping in
long rain that sounds as if strained through silk   letting fall
heavy drops of light

JULY   *giyo giyo*

trees buzz, peony cacti burn with colour, cicadas screech and
screech   as soon as the summer showers pass   and the
night dew dissolves the distant mountain shadows   *giyo
giyo*   frogs' voices start to overwhelm the universe   as
the moon climbs it rises to *gyawaro gyawaro rororori*   a vast
chorus for the poet Shimpei

AUGUST   *kana kana kana*

a century slowly sets   whirling cumulonimbus light
playing like a silver instrument   *kana kana kana kana*
nails of cicadas' voices thinly pierce the moonset air   quiv-
ering the cooling grove

93

SEPTEMBER   *ririririri*

ririririri......riri,   ririri......ririri,   riri......ri,   riririri......
are these insects singing in the grass?   or a ringing in
the ears?   month of the long moon   lengthening
nights   the moon illuminating a dark night's dreams of
pampas grass

OCTOBER   *kasakoso*

the dark blue sky stretching to that other world   when
scattered showers have skimmed over   northern uplands'
wasabi-coloured woods   countless thousands of folding
fans dance   the tree-tops begin to brighten   on the
ground, *kasakoso*, a faint sound, indicating   a scuttling
mouse's footsteps?   an earthquake's whisper?

NOVEMBER   *saku saku*

morning frost *tatami* in the frost-month   walking
along the mountain paths paved with withered leaves, *sari*
sari   walking across the tangled waves of white hair fields,
saku saku   countless needles of ice split and shatter   the
clear air's serene *s*-sounds   like the snap of biting a green
apple

DECEMBER   *shin shin*

shin shin   no lull in the December sky   the white-
patterned bamboo blinds come down   as the snow falls, *shin*
shin   lighting a lamp under eaves   people fix their gaze
on what cannot be seen   *shin shin shin shin*   that is the
sound of time passing away   *shin shin shin shin*   and
thus thousands of years pass away

THE FIRST EMPEROR, 2003

Naka's nō play concerns the first emperor of China, Shi Huangdi (259–210 BCE), whose name literally means 'The First Emperor'. He unified the country by founding the Qin dynasty in 221 BCE. Sima Qian's *The Historical Records* relates how, after becoming emperor, he had a number of border walls joined together to form what is now known as the Great Wall of China, all previous works of literature destroyed, and hundreds of Confucian scholars executed. In his quest for immortality, he sent a sorcerer named Xu Fu on an expedition to Mount Penglai, a mythical mountain said to exist across the sea to the east of China in a land called Fusang. He also ordered the construction of a magnificent mausoleum for himself at the foot of Mount Li to the north-east of his capital, Xianyang, near the modern-day city of Xi'an. Some of the terracotta warriors built to guard this mausoleum were discovered in 1974 and form the 'ghostly army' that appears at the start of the play.

The stage of the National Noh Theatre, Tokyo, where *The First Emperor* was first performed. The chorus sits on the main stage (house right), the flute-player and the drummers sit at the back of the stage under the painted pine tree, and the actors enter across the bridge (house left).

THE FIRST EMPEROR

I

Darkness.

The chorus, the subterranean army of the First Emperor's tomb, floats up quietly.

CHORUS:

> Some twenty miles from the eastern suburbs of Xi'an,
> rising out of the billowing yellow dust,
> the ghostly army appears.
>
> Leading the lines, sixty-eight men, then three ranks of two
>   hundred men or more
> carrying quivers, their hands holding bows.
>
> Behind them, between the walls,
> four orderly columns of troops,
>
> soldiers wearing blue-grey light outer robes,
>
> soldiers wearing dark brown plated armour,
>
> young soldiers, middle-aged soldiers, old soldiers:
>
> gaping mouth, thick lips and large forehead, a guileless one
>
>   (he seems to be from Guanzhong in Qin)
>
> round cheeks and pointed chin, an agile one
>
>   (he seems to be a warrior from Bashu)

small pupils, narrow eyes and high cheekbones, a fearless
    one

    (he is perhaps from Longdong)

or there, a piercing gaze, white moustache, the stately
    general

        (he must have performed great deeds to reach his
            position)

infantry, horses, chariots, and archers,
cavalry, heralds, guardsmen and commanders

and, protecting the emperor, dispassionate, the imperial
    guard
with cavalry, chariots, some seven or eight thousand
    of them,

many still in the land of yellow earth
across two thousand two hundred years

some standing up,

some lying down;

either facing up to the heavens,

or facing the earth;

some have lost their heads,

some their arms;

they wake from their sleep of eternal suspense.

What is it they declaim?

Fade into darkness.

2

Xu Fu's descendant appears on the bridge.

XU FU'S DESCENDANT:

Time comes   and goes,
people appear   and disappear;
earth and sky where all things briefly stay
are nothing but a temporary home.
Days and months are travellers of eternity,
so are the years that pass by;
time wanders astray and returns.

I am a traveller come from a distant island in the eastern
        seas.
I am a descendant of Xu Fu, who was asked by the First
        Emperor
more than seventy generations and two thousand years ago
to seek the Elixir of Life on the island of Penglai.
I have come to visit Xianyang's ancient castle.
I do not even know where the old capital lies, nor can the
        things of the past be seen.
When I wandered further to the east,

from out of the billowing yellow dust
I saw the ghostly army gradually appearing

like a day-dream.

The chorus at the back of the stage begins to sing.

CHORUS:

> We are those who died in the Emperor's quest for
> immortality.
>
> We are those who were ordered to guard the Emperor's
> eternal life.
>
> Before, the Emperor cut down an enemy force of hundreds
> of thousands,
>
> gathered the *Book of Odes*, the *Book of Classics*, and the
> works of all the sages   and had them burnt to
> ashes,
>
> had more than four hundred and sixty Confucian scholars
> buried alive
>
> and all the while the Emperor   ardently searched for
> his own immortality.
>
> He ascended the throne at thirteen years old;
>
> soon he began to construct his burial mound on Mount Li,
> to build a magnificent underground palace.
> Seven hundred thousand from across the empire were set to
> work;
> palaces for a hundred officials were created;
> the tomb was filled with rare and valuable treasures;
> to avoid decay a hundred rivers and a great sea of mercury
> were formed;
> and candles were lit made of wax from the fat of mermaids
> that was designed to burn for ever

and he had a hundred and twenty thousand wealthy
    households transferred there;

three thousand beautiful women were installed in the
    rear palace;

ten thousand miles of wall   and the Epang Palace
    were constructed;

within the mound's two-hundred-mile perimeter, two
    hundred and seventy towers were linked;

and he toured the lands he had subjugated.

The light changes.

3

The day-dream of Xu Fu's descendant.

*Drawn by the sound of the musicians, the First Emperor, ruler of
all nations under heaven, and a minister appear.*

THE FIRST EMPEROR:

An illusory dream, an illusory dream is this world.
Drawn on by four horses,
the golden chariot's wheels grind on,
leaving Xianyang
with firm purpose, setting out to the east.
When heaven and the four directions are governed
we'll go on endlessly through broad fields
cut through dark tangled forests

clamber steep rocky slopes
whose surfaces resemble giant elephants
and on the sacred peak of Taishan
perform the ritual conferring divinity.

THE FIRST EMPEROR AND MINISTER:

After dawn the burning clouds
are redder than fire-flames
and the colour of the grass and trees brightens,
lighter than mist.

THE FIRST EMPEROR:

When I rub my hips on the pine's roots,
its thousand years of jade green fill the world.

MINISTER:

The dark sea is like molten gold,
the crowd of mountains resembles painted brows.

CHORUS:

Standing upon the Langya plateau,
facing Fusang in the distant east,
on the other side of the glittering sea,
reaching the rainbow's steps,
an illusory dream, an illusory dream:
we have set eyes on the Jewelled Isle.

MINISTER:

His rule is now complete. I cannot match His Majesty's light;
even I am pacified.

ATTENDANT:

Many are the blessings of this Sovereign,

MINISTER:

I can only revere His Majesty.

Xu Fu of the past appears.

XU FU:

How might I speak with His Majesty?

ATTENDANT:

Who are you who seek to speak with His Majesty?

XU FU:

I am Xu Fu from near the Langya plateau.

ATTENDANT:

Well then, what do you wish to say to His Majesty?

XU FU:

I wish to offer His Majesty the Elixir of Eternal Life.

ATTENDANT:

Please wait a moment while I speak with His Majesty,

Attendant moves to centre stage.

ATTENDANT:

May I speak with His Majesty? A man who lives in this area has come here to say something to His Majesty.

MINISTER:

Well then, let him come here and speak.

ATTENDANT:

Thank you.

The attendant faces Xu Fu.

ATTENDANT:

I have explained the reason you came. You may go in.

Xu Fu faces the First Emperor and bends his head down deeply.

XU FU:

On the other side of the sea lie the Three Sacred Mountains of Penglai, Fangzhang, and Yingzhou. The sacred hermits live there; it is said that they possess the medicine that can prolong life. I wish to make preparations and search for it, then bring it as an offering to Your Majesty.

THE FIRST EMPEROR:

Ever since I first longed for the rainbow's steps and the mysterious visions of those green sacred mountains, I have been consumed by my desire to obtain the medicine that prolongs life.

Can you really go there and obtain it for me?

XU FU:

I can. I wish to request three thousand young boys and girls and a few hundred ships for the journey.

THE FIRST EMPEROR:

In that case, in addition to three thousand young boys and girls, you shall be provided with five varieties of grain, agricultural tools, and containers for them.

Xu Fu respectfully withdraws and exits.

THE FIRST EMPEROR:

The sea is so vast, the winds so strong.

CHORUS:

Clouds and waves   gather in misty distance,
seemingly endless   and unfathomable;
unfathomably deep, Xu Fu's eyes darkly mirror the cosmos.
We cannot not believe him,
though we do not believe him.
Will he bring back the Elixir of Life?
Do the rainbow's steps or those green mountains really exist?
No, they will all turn out to be illusions.

As the chorus sings, the First Emperor exits.

(INTERMISSION.)

4

Evening. Xu Fu's descendant quietly sings.

XU FU'S DESCENDANT:

> Green, green, the grass, the sunlight pale,
> vast, vast, the earth, the wind cold.
> Green and vast, the foot of Mount Li,
> where could it be, the Emperor's grave?
> Pity vainly entwines the ivy,
> countless shapes sadly darken.

Led by the sound of the musicians, the First Emperor's spirit appears on the bridge.

THE FIRST EMPEROR'S SPIRIT:

> Fierce, fierce the winds, never stopping,
> time never ceases, whirling round and round.
> I have been waiting so long for Xu Fu to return –
> but will he return, or not? The white waves
> of doubt come crashing in, come crashing in;
> the desire for eternal life is vain.
> Two thousand miles from the capital, Xianyang,
> I died on the road at Shaqiu Pingtai.
> Each accompanying wagon carried a barrel of salted fish
> in order to hide the smell of my corpse;
> I was brought back secretly to the capital, and buried in
>> Mount Li.

CHORUS:

> To defend his deep underground palace,
> eight thousand of us motionless cavalry were deployed.

The impregnability of his underground palace,
his own immortality, did he believe these in the end?
Did he truly believe us, his soldier guards?

The First Emperor's spirit moves to centre stage.

THE FIRST EMPEROR'S SPIRIT:

No, I do not believe these things.
I have lost my belief in anything in the world.
I cannot even believe my own birth.
My father later became King Zhuangxiang of Qin.
When he was a hostage to the Kingdom of Zhao, he was
        named Zichu,
but my mother, Yang Zhai, was the great merchant Lü
        Buwei's concubine.
My father asked to be given her, but she may have already
        been pregnant.
Moreover, after she was given to my father, Lü often came
        to visit her.
There's nothing to say Lü Buwei isn't my father.
I gave him the Kingdom of Xiang and called him 'Uncle',
but did he selflessly perform his duties for me as for a
        superior,
or did he secretly love me as his son? I cannot know.
Later I had Lü Buwei stripped of his posts and banished,
but in the land of his banishment he took poison and
        committed suicide.

The chorus speaks.

CHORUS:

If he were my real father, then I have killed my own father,
but I have no regrets, I do not know what is bad

107

and what is good in this world.
I do not believe in right or wrong, good or bad. There is no
    absolute good,
so nothing can be bad.
If you perceive something to be good, it is good. If you
    decide something is bad, it is bad.
What decides whether it is good or bad is power only,
so I sought power only, I had to become the eternal ruler.
Vassals serve for power only, their hearts cannot be trusted.

THE FIRST EMPEROR'S SPIRIT:

Xu Fu claimed he would seek the Elixir of Life,
for which he requested tremendous resources and left for
    Penglai Island.
But he never returned, and disappeared without trace.
Did he plan to escape Qin and go into exile?
Did he trick me into believing in a potion that did not
    exist?

In the dream, Xu Fu's descendant changes into Xu Fu himself.

XU FU:

I did not trick the Emperor.
I did not seek to escape by going to the Land of Penglai.
I could not reach Penglai Island to seek the Elixir of Life;
I climbed steep mountains and entered dark valleys, I
    searched caverns no one had ever entered,
but I could not find it in the end,
so at last I have come to realise
the vanity of searching for the Elixir of Life.

CHORUS:

From the wavering of *mu* all things come into being,
and all things that are must soon return to *mu*.
All things in the cosmos move from *mu* to *mu*.
Human lives are no exception.
Ageing and death belong to life's process.
All blooming flowers, all treasures, are nothing more than
    castles in the sky.
Every desire and illusion, like the rainbow's steps,
vanishes half-way through in the mist.

XU FU:

Even the pine that lasts a thousand years will rot.
Though it lives for just a day, the rose mallow still blooms,
at last I have come to realise
the vanity of craving for longevity.

THE FIRST EMPEROR'S SPIRIT:

I have found the same to be true.
Though once in Xianyang, when spring was at its peak,
the palace garden's golden willows streamed,
a hundred officials accompanied me in the Jewelled Tower
    Palace,
and three thousand beauties attended me in the Women's
    Quarters,
time moves and the stars change;
now there is nothing to support me.

CHORUS:

To seek a permanent world on earth, building an under-
    ground palace,

though you make a hundred mercury rivers and an ocean of
mercury flow, in the end it is vanity.
though you burn candles made from the wax of mermaids,
now darkness returns.

THE FIRST EMPEROR'S SPIRIT:

Three thousand worlds dissolved before the eyes.

CHORUS:

Eighty-four thousand phenomena utterly vanished.

The First Emperor's spirit performs the Dance of the Rainbow's Steps.

THE FIRST EMPEROR'S SPIRIT:

The limitless thirst for power,
the search for eternal life.

CHORUS:

Still the limitless thirst for power diminishes, with green
waves, into the distance;
still the search for eternal life stretches on, like white mist,
without end.
Still the Emperor's unappeasable spirit
on the far shore of burning dreams
burning dreams
climbs the rainbow's steps,
climbs the rainbow's steps,
mingles with the clouds of the great void,
and turns into cosmic dust,
and turns into cosmic dust.

The First Emperor's spirit exits along the bridge through the curtain.

Xu Fu's descendant remains on the stage alone; the voices of the chorus echo to silence.

NOTES FOR A POETICS, 1966

1

What is poetry? That is something no-one can define. It is only possible to try and gesture towards it. To indicate something that is indefinable might seem a contradiction, but it is rather because it cannot be defined that it can be indicated, and it is because of this that poems are written.

A poem is always an experiment, and a poetics is another kind of experiment. There is a necessary difference between the two. Perhaps it is because of this difference that each can have its meaning: if they were identical, one would become redundant.

This essay is, however, merely a modest personal reflection. There is nothing original here. I must return to confirm for myself what is self-evident to others.

2

The fundamental motives for the activity of creating poetry are obscure. At least at first glance, it has no visible purpose or reason. There have never been as many writers arming them-selves with social purposes and goals to justify the creation of their poems as there are today, but is the activity of creating poetry not rather at root a very personal one that turns away from society?

Creating poetry cannot be replaced by, nor can it replace, any other activity. Moreover, it is because the desire to create poetry cannot be fulfilled by any other activity that poems are created. It springs from an unmistakable internal desire that has no direct relationship with the everyday world. It is because of a wish not to silence this desire but to fulfil it that one writes.

3

The activity of writing is itself, of course, a visible activity. One holds a pen, faces the paper, and in everyday time moves one's own hand. However, what one's consciousness works to indicate certainly does not take place in the visible world, but in a separate, unreal one. In this unreal space, through using those unreal 'things', words, one acts in order to reach (an indefinable) something.

The activity of creating poetry is always an escape to this unreal space.

4

What to write? One cannot say this in advance. To say that thought should precede, or perhaps follow, the creation of poetry, that it is at the very heart of the activity of creating poetry, and that the writer is obliged to discuss it, is tedious. Trying to state something for the purpose of what has already been decided upon is to turn writing into a means, and cannot truly be called writing.

In writing, a writer should not aim for assertion, judgement, confession – or any kind of self-expression. To write in order to state something is nothing more than propaganda. To write in order to state something more effectively can be classed as being no more than rhetoric or oratory. By contrast, true writing is none other than the seeking of writing, nothing more than seeking what you seek. It is not oratory as a means but, rather, oratory itself.

The attitude that the writer should then adopt is – whether it is truly possible or not is another matter – the complete relinquishment of the existing self.

5

To make the self disappear by confronting words: not to use words as instruments for stating something, but to attend to words as 'things', has to stem from this.

6

For the writer of poetry, the meaning of writing resides, perhaps, in the action of writing itself. This self-sufficiency is equal to 'play'. The work that has finished being written is no more than the product of this action.

The meaning of writing and the meaning that the written work suggests must not be confused. They are two completely different things.

7

Is the work only a product? Perhaps, but then again, it cannot be denied that the writer desires the work. To say that the meaning of doing resides in the action of doing it itself is certainly not to say that the born or created thing's meaning can be denied. It is rather the opposite. It is because one cannot acknowledge the born or created thing as paramount that one must go back to the action of writing itself.

The *actual* work is always only secondary. Because of this, the significance of the action of writing comes back to the fore. If it achieves perfection, does the action of writing itself not disappear?

The fact that the writer desires the actual work, which is only secondary, perhaps only shows the writer's *actual* powerlessness. The work is always a form of renunciation.

8

The secondary, but actual, work. That is all that one can create. That is why one cannot but call it a work. At least, one wishes to let these illusory petals float on in the emptiness.

9

What the written work is, the writer cannot say. The work's existence always surpasses the writer. Undoubtedly, the work exists as something constructed by the words themselves, but while it is something uttered by the writer, it is not his possession, because its existence surpasses the writer. The writer certainly cannot know the work itself. He can only create it.

The work has its own independence; it has a transcendental existence. Thus, as a phenomenon, and also for the writer himself, it is always something that wavers and does not remain still.

As an object, the work wavers and does not remain still because the work awaits a reader (the receiving subject) to compose it; the reader always creates the work as a new phenomenon.

So the writer, too, after finishing writing, is just another reader.

10

The 'poetry' of a poem cannot be named or defined. In response to this, many use the epithet 'poetic' for this unnamable and undefinable thing.

The poetic work does not deny meaning; it is always pregnant with unlimited meanings. It is like water reflecting. It does not reflect the writer but, rather, each individual reader. The work is not the writer himself; each reader has to be something both substantial and transparent so that he can create meaning.

However, writers often appropriate words and limit the work by simply turning them into instruments of self-depiction.

11

The writer does not write for the sake of something he wished to state beforehand. It should be said that it is because the writer does not know what he should say that he writes, and that it is because the writer struggles to write that he wants to write.

However, the work is necessarily cut off from the writer and *surpasses* him. The work is therefore not closed; it is open. By the action of reading, the reader makes the meaning exist.

The writer must not intend the work as self-expression. The work simply seeks to be a work in itself. Here a person does not state something but, rather, the words themselves come to appear via that person. However, if the reader reads this as something that *has been expressed*, the writer cannot avoid it. The work does not remain in the possession of the writer; however, it also cannot be avoided that the reader makes assumptions and hypotheses about the writer via the work.

The work, constructed with impersonal words, cannot be equated with the writer, and this should not be sought either. On the other hand, however, it is perhaps impossible for the tint of a writer's spirit not to leave its trace on the reader. The writer always belongs to the work.

12

What makes the work come into being is not the writer's individuality, experience, thought, or feeling. It is only through words, whose existence is transcendent for the writer, that the work comes into being.

13

Language fundamentally cannot be a reflection of reality in itself. Words, the units of language, are no more than abstract signs. These do indeed refer to things and phenomena, but what appears from this reference does so only due to the receiving subject's imagining consciousness. What appears – 現出 (*genshutsu*) – is certainly not reality in itself. It would be better to call it 幻出 (*genshutsu*): the appearance of illusion.

Words, or language, are at root unnatural and unreal. They are none other than illusory appearances which depend on the vanishing of the object.

Consequently, it goes without saying that the writer must strongly deny as a delusion the possibility that the referential function of the language in his work can be equated with real objects, and that he should be concerned only to allow illusions to arise.

Moreover, the writer cannot restrict or limit the illusions that are thus allowed to arise. Words do not belong to the writer, because they belong to language. They are therefore entrusted to each particular receiver's imagining consciousness.

The writer can only clarify, as precisely as he can, the structure of words as devices for making what is invisible appear.

14

The action of writing is always an intention to reach an unreal space.

That is, however, first made possible by the existence of those unreal 'things', words; without words, it is impossible to breathe in this unreal space.

What gives words their function as words is, it goes without saying, their reception by a receiving subject.

In that case, can the action of writing be possible without thinking about the receiving subject (the reader)?

To write also means to entrust oneself to words and to the reader.

The notion that writing is an abandoning of the self for the writer must stem from this.

15

The language in a poetic work cannot merely be based on words' function as indicators of objects, or of the function of metaphorical meaning which arises from that. It must be based as closely as possible on the structure of words as thing-like existences with visual form and with sound.

To seek the autonomous order of words themselves as 'things': this is what the writer of poetry follows as he creates.

At the same time it reveals, perhaps necessarily, the writer's own inner order.

16

Words possess, through their written form and their sound, a thing-like existence.

Just as a stone has a thing-like existence, a word has one too. However, this is certainly not to deny a word's function as an abstract sign.

At the same time as words are abstract signs with the function of indicating objects, they are themselves 'things' that are visual and phonetic objects.

Through this operation, this duality of words – these fundamentally different functions of words as signs and as 'thingness' – can be at times estranged and separate, but they can also frequently overlap and intersect with one another.

Always to measure and objectify this relationship between the two: through the reader, these two are picked up in combination in the blink of an eye. However, the writer must, as carefully as possible, be analytically aware of this.

17

For example, the image of a stone as a physical object and the image resulting from the word 'stone' itself are certainly not the same. Of course, through the word 'stone' functioning as a sign indicating an object, it brings up the image of a stone as a physical object. At the same time, however, it also possesses the image brought up by the written form itself of 'stone', the image brought up by the sound of 'stone' and, moreover, the image built up from the associations the word itself has acquired over time. This is no different from what is commonly referred to as the sense of a word.

Although the sensation given by a stone itself and the sensation of the word 'stone' are not completely unrelated, they are clearly different things.

To take at will an unsophisticated example, if 右 (*migi*, 'right') is suggested by the word 石 (*ishi*, 'stone'), this is, it goes without saying, not due to the stone as a physical object, but to its written form, and if 西 (*nishi*, 'west') is suggested by the word 石 (*ishi*, 'stone'), it is due to the 'ishi' sound. To give yet another example, if 白い (*shiroi*, 'white') is suggested, is this due not to the stone as a really existing physical object, but rather to Bashō's hokku, *Ishiyama no ishi yori shiroshi aki no kaze* ('Whiter than the stones of Ishiyama temple – the wind in autumn')? Even if, in this case, the reader does not know about the real Ishiyama, on reflection this is no hindrance.

In this way, the word 'stone' is independent of the stone itself as a physical object, and being itself a 'thing', gains its own autonomous existence.

18

The idea that words are 'things' is easily misunderstood. Words as 'things' do not have no meaning. That is, they are meaningful on a different level from that of words used merely as a sign indicating an object.

Generally speaking, no 'things' can be divested of meaning. Rather, one perhaps cannot grasp 'things' without them having meaning.

To take the stone as an example, doesn't everyone consider it to have meaning? For instance, it is an obstruction on a road or a train track, or it is a weight on a pickle barrel; by having a relationship or use in people's everyday reality, these are of course a kind of meaning. On the other hand, when examined as simply a sensory object removed from all its everyday relationships and uses, it appeals to one's aesthetic feeling (regardless of whether it is felt to be beautiful or ugly) and thus calls up a kind of psychological response, that stone must obtain another meaning that is different from that of its everyday use.

In the same way, through this 'thingness' of words, when grasped as visual form or as sound, the words appeal to one's perception or aesthetic feeling, provoke the imagining consciousness, and awaken latent memories or associations; moreover, it is by words being 'things' that they have meaning on a different level from their meanings as signs.

19

Words, which appear with the disappearance of the object, are given meaning by the receiving subject, who does so by erasing their 'thingness'. One does not look at the word itself as a 'thing', but at its image. One does not hear the sound of the word as 'thing', but the sound's 'image'.

By their being 'things', words have a metaphysical existence, and it is through such an existence that they are unreal 'things'.

20

The words in a poetic work are not simply a means for transmitting logical or conceptual meaning; rather, this meaning-making itself has its own purpose: it expresses the existence of meaning-making *itself*.

The 'meaning' referred to here does not in fact exist, but rather is created as a *phenomenon* by the receiving subject. Therefore it cannot be completely limited. However, this does not mean, of course, that it is completely unlimited either. It is placed by the writer and, through the relational construction of words, is shown as something whose directions are clearly channelled. The reader, adapting to such construction, has the freedom to produce according to what is received. This freedom, however, is demarcated by his sensibility, latent memories, imaginative power, thoughts, feelings – above all his *linguistic experience*.

Moreover, an external factor that largely demarcates this is the quantity of the word's own linguistic experience arising within its language system's socio-historical production.

21

The meaning of a word as 'thing' – a word's smell, its nuance, the so-called 'word-spirit' (*kotodama*)– arises from its visual form and its sound, but on the other hand, its character is also produced by the socio-historical accumulations of its cultural formation. Therefore, at the same time as being something directly perceived, it is also above all something traditional. A word's latent energy is none other than what is formed by the interconnection between the words in a work's construction as a whole, but these possibilities are already the almost objective possession of the word's socio-historical production.

Words are, to put it bluntly, culture itself, tradition itself. It could almost be said that words (*kotoba*) are *kotodama*, the spirit of words. Therefore, their translation into another language system as they are is *fundamentally* impossible. Words as 'things' are certainly not the universal 'things' that can cross the borders of a language system.

22

There is no such thing as the pure sound of the word itself.

For example, the onomatopoeia *shin shin* in *shin shin to yuki ga furu* (the snow falls *shin shin*) immediately calls to mind a psychological response. To a Japanese, it would be impossible to hear the sound *shin shin* cut off from this response. But this is something that operates within one language system, and in another language system, it would be impossible to have such a response. If an American were to lament the impossibility of its translation, our response must be that that goes without saying.

Similarly, for example, although the onomatopoeia *nuru nuru*'s 'word-spirit' recalls a slimy sensation, it is something only possible for Japanese; the same cannot be expected of a non-Japanese.

As a further example, the difference between flowers scattering *hira hira* and scattering *hara hara*, all too clear to a Japanese, certainly does not *just* depend on the difference in sound itself. Non-Japanese really cannot perceive the difference in their 'word-feel'.

In this way, even in the case of onomatopoeia, there cannot be a universally transmissible pure sound; in these very cases, the 'sound-image' is only sufficient within a single language system.

NOTE: It could be that the *shin shin* above, if we trace it back to its root, is not Japanese onomatopoeia but, rather, originates from the Chinese 涔涔 ('rain rain', *cén cén* in modern Mandarin, *shin shin* in Japanese transcription) or 深深 ('deep deep', *shēn shēn* in modern Mandarin, *shin shin* in Japanese transcription). However, at least in the linguistic consciousness of today's Japanese, not in the association of the word but the *association of the sound*, it has been made into a Japanese onomatopoeia.

23

The sound of a word (*kotoba*) is the echo (*kodama*) of the word-spirit (*kotodama*). Perhaps in its most basic sense, it is the life of a word, which arouses people's distant latent consciousness and associations cultivated by tradition and has the power to appeal to deep-seated feelings. Words divested of their 'sound-image' are no more than stuffed specimens of language; in the case of written words, sounds function as auditory impressions.

The visual image of words requires the alteration of sound into space.

24

The play of sounds between words – above all, the search for assonant or alliterative words. This is not simply the technique of aiming for beautiful sound effects. The writer does not seek these effects, but rather follows the words' autonomous movement with an empty mind. By one word calling up another, by moving from one word onto another, you reach unforeseen places. Therefore, without being constrained by the overt logic of syntax, it is almost as if the words speak of their own accord, rolling on like waves, one after another. This is, however, perhaps a very different thing from surrealism's automatic writing. Here there is not the licence of the erasure of diffusion of consciousness; with extreme concentration of consciousness, the writer is *made* to choose the words. Even when breaking the boundaries of logic, your consciousness always has to be awake.

25

The fundamental motives for the activity of creating poetry are obscure. The agent of this activity cannot express this. A work has no such thing as a subject matter. One can only say that the writing of the work itself is, for him, the subject matter. Because writing is precisely to be guided by words, to accompany words to where they go, if there is something that the words themselves show, it is nothing other than this itself that constitutes the work's subject matter.

Poetic works are not directly written to someone. One should say, rather, that they are an offering to the vaster *mu* that lies beyond ourselves.

However, it cannot be denied that, whether or not the writer himself is aware of it, by concerning himself with 'words', he concerns himself with his culture and tradition. Why is it that he is possessed by words and cannot survive without them?

In the act of writing, he does not take part in 'reality' or society. Rather, he writes in order to escape. Yet why does he desire his own work, become almost obsessed by it? The written work, whether he loves it or hates it, has a real existence, a social existence; there is no other place where it could exist.

MARCH 1966

NOTES

Japanese Authors, Artists, Literary Works, & Historical Figures

ANZAI HITOSHI (1919–1994): post-war poet. The poem alluded to in 'Passing Shower Thoughts' is 'Night Shower', which opens with a description of Tokyo's zinc roofs.

EBIHARA KINOSUKE (1904–1970): Japanese expressionist painter especially active in Paris in the 1920s.

BASHŌ: Matsuo Bashō (1644–1694): the most renowned haikai poet in Japan. (The term 'haiku' only came into general use in the late nineteenth century.)

BONCHŌ: Nozawa Bonchō (1640–1714): haikai poet and disciple of Bashō.

BUSON: Yosa Buson (1716–1784): painter, and one of the most famous Japanese haikai poets.

HAGIWARA SAKUTARŌ (1886–1942): major Japanese poet whose work was an important influence on Naka. His first free-verse collection, *Howling at the Moon*, was published in 1917.

JŌSŌ: Naitō Jōsō (1662–1704): haikai poet and disciple of Bashō.

KATŌ SHŪICHI (1919–2008): leading Japanese intellectual and haiku poet.

KOKINSHŪ ('Collection of the Past and Present'): tenth-century imperially commissioned anthology of Japanese poetry edited by the waka poet Ki no Tsurayuki (872–945).

KUSANO SHIMPEI (1903–1988): poet well-known for his book *Frogs*, which was awarded the Yomiuri Prize in 1949. Some of his poems were translated by Cid Corman under the title *Selected Frogs* in 1963.

KYORAI: Mukai Kyorai (1651–1704): haikai poet and disciple of Bashō.

MANYŌSHŪ ('Collection of Ten Thousand Leaves'): eighth-century anthology of Japanese poetry, generally considered with the tenth-century *Kokinshū* to be the greatest in the history of Japanese poetry.

MINAMOTO NO SANETOMO (1192–1219): famous waka poet. His collection of waka, *Collection of the Kamakura Minister*, is believed to have been composed in 1213.

ONO NO OYU (?–737): poet whose poems appear in the *Manyōshū*.

SHINKOKINSHŪ ('New Collection of the Past and Present'): imperially commissioned anthology of Japanese poetry completed in 1205 and edited by six prominent poets of the time, one of whom was Fujiwara no Ietaka (1158–1237).

SHINSHOKUKOKINSHŪ ('New Collection of the Past and Present Continued'): the last imperially commissioned Japanese poetry anthology, completed in 1439 and edited by Asukai Masayo (1390–1452).

SHŌTETSU (1381–1459): often considered the last major waka poet before the late-nineteenth-century reforms of Masaoka Shiki (1867–1902). His fifteen-volume *Collection of Grass Roots,* gathering more than eleven thousand waka, was edited shortly after his death by one of his disciples.

SŌGI (1421–1502): waka and renga poet. *His Journey Along the Tsukushi Road* is an account of his travels to Western Japan.

TAIRA NO KIYOMORI (1118–1181): well-known military leader who features in *The Tale of the Heike.*

THE TALE OF GENJI: novel written in the early eleventh century by Murasaki Shikibu (c. 970–c. 1019).

THE TALE OF THE HEIKE: epic mediaeval account of the war between the Taira and Minamoto clans in 1180–1185.

THE TALES OF ISE: collection of waka poems embedded in a series of tales. Its dates of composition and editorship are unknown, but it is often dated to the late ninth century.

TOYOTOMI HIDEYOSHI (1537–1598): military leader who unified the country following the 'Warring States' period of the late sixteenth century.

YAMANOUE NO OKURA (C. 660–C. 733): poet whose poems appear in the *Manyōshū*.

Notes

POEM I: *w h i s p e r*: In the original Japanese, the conventional vertical layout of the poem's lines changes to a horizontal one for this final word of the poem, with each syllable appearing in a separate line. Rather than reversing this shift from the vertical to the horizontal and presenting 'whisper' as a vertical line in English, we have kept the final word's layout horizontal because we interpreted Naka's choice as imitative of the jellyfish being washed ashore.

MIST: *Urashima's box* refers to the traditional Japanese legend of Urashima Tarō, a fisherman who rescues a turtle and, as a reward, is brought by the turtle to the Dragon Palace. He spends what he thinks are only a few days there but when he returns to his village, three hundred years have passed. When he opens the box he was not supposed to open, he becomes an old man.

NOTE TO MUSIC: for further discussion of the term *mu*, see pages 13–14 of the Introduction.

HAKATA I: AFTERWORD *&* NOTES
Who is it the sailors long for? Listening to plaintive voices in Ōshima Bay: from Edward Seidensticker's translation of *The Tale of Genji*.
Chikuzen: the old province in which Hakata was situated.
…the yū *('evening') of* yūyami *('evening darkness') puns on the homophonous* iu *('to say')*: we have tried to render this elsewhere in the line through the 'say' sound embedded within 'vexation'.
cogon-grass: traditionally, people pass through cogon-grass rings in shrines during the summer to bring good health.
Umi no Nakamichi ('Path through the Sea'): the name of the tombolo linking Shika Island to the mainland near Hakata.
Sumiyoshi Shrine: according to folklore, Empress Jingū gave Sumiyoshi its name by declaring that the area there was

sumiyoshi, 'a good place to live'. The *uta* and Naka's poem pun on this folk-etymology. *Records of the Origins of Sumiyoshi Shrine* is said to date from the eighth century.

Sokotsutsu-no-o / Nakatsutsu-no-o / Uwatsutsu-no-o: *soko, naka* and *uwa* refer respectively to the bottom, middle and surface of the sea. The origin of *tsutsu* is disputed, but Ueda Masaaki claims it is related to *tsu* ('port'). *No* is a possessive particle; *o* can mean 'man'. Thus, they are sea-gods. They were later also treated as a single 'Sumiyoshi deity'. Sumiyoshi, once also called Suminoe, now lies a little inland in Ōsaka, but in ancient times it was an important trading port, and Sumiyoshi Shrine has long been a place to pray for a safe sea voyage.

a horse gallops out of the gap towards the evening: the 'white horse' may be related to the 'white horse festival', held just after the New Year at Sumiyoshi Shrine to pray for good health and for the country's prosperity.

At Suma, melancholy autumn winds were blowing: from Edward Seidensticker's translation of *The Tale of Genji*.

Ply over ply of white clouds scattering in the land of Tsukushi: the line puns on *tsukushi*, which, as well as being the older name for Kyūshū, the island on which Naka was born, means (with a different Chinese character) 'to use up' or 'expend'.

OPUS**: *omnia mutantur, nihil interit*: 'Everything changes, nothing dies', a Latin saying found in Ovid's *Metamorphoses*, where it is spoken by Pythagoras.

OLD-STYLE OLD POND SONNET: *suffering walnut*: The Japanese original's alliterative *kurushimi no kurumi* ('suffering walnut' or 'walnut of suffering') likely alludes to Hiraide Takashi's *For the Fighting Spirit of the Walnut*, particularly its closing section, in which 'the walnut suffers' (*kurumi ga kurushimu*). Hiraide's collection appeared three years before *No-Self Mountain Temple Diary and Other Poems* and was translated by Sawako Nakayasu in 2008.

DREAM • MEMORY: *Paul Delvaux* (1897–1994): Belgian painter associated with surrealism during the 1920s.

JULY: *Gion Yamakasa festival*: a festival held over the first two weeks of July in Hakata. It is said to have begun during an epidemic in 1241 when the Buddhist monk Enni (1202–1280) was carried through Hakata and sprinkled it with holy water. One of the first stages of the festival involves the fetching of purifying sand from the nearby beach at Hakozaki and bringing it back to Hakata. Gion derives from the similar Gion festival in the Kyoto district of that name; *Yamakasa* refer to the large floats that are run through the streets of Hakata at the festival's conclusion. These lines also evoke the famous opening of the fourteenth-century *The Tale of the Heike*: 'The sound of Gion monastery's bells echoes the impermanence of all things'.

the author of 'Spinning Gears' drank Veronal: Akutagawa Ryūnosuke (1892–1927), a prominent Taishō-era author, committed suicide on 24 July 1927 by taking a fatal dose of the sleeping aid Veronal. The short story 'Spinning Gears' was published posthumously.

PASSER-BY: *a hokku by the haikai master born in Kema village*: Yosa Buson. Before Masaoka Shiki (1867–1902) popularised the term 'haiku', the genre was generally called 'haikai', and the initial poem of a linked 'haikai' sequence a 'hokku' ('starting verse'). Naka is careful to use the correct terms for Buson's time.

SEASON-WORD GLOSSARY OF SOUNDS

Musashino's snowbell blossoms: Musashino is the Tokyo suburb in which Naka lived at the time of this poem's composition.

Tsukushi's soapberry blossoms: Tsukushi is an old name for the island of Kyūshū, where Naka was born.

Ogasawara's wiliwili blossoms: the tropical Ogasawara Islands are a group of Japanese islands situated around a thousand kilometres south of Tokyo.

Kisakata's silktree blossoms: Kisakata is a town in Akita Prefecture, northern Japan.

THE FIRST EMPEROR

Guanzhong in Qin: an area belonging to the Qin bordering the Wei and Yellow Rivers.

Bashu: an old name for the area roughly corresponding to modern Sichuan Province, which was conquered by the Qin over the course of the third century BCE.

Longdong: a town in modern-day western Sichuan.

the land of yellow earth: China.

Xu Fu: a sorcerer for the First Emperor who was sent, as the play indicates, to look for the Elixir of Life in the eastern seas.

Days and months are travellers of eternity: an allusion to the opening sentence of Matsuo Bashō's *The Narrow Road to the Interior*.

Penglai: a mythical island to the east of China where eternal life was to be found.

Xianyang: the capital of the state of Qin.

Before, the Emperor cut down an enemy force of hundreds of thousands: during the First Emperor's unification of China in 221 BCE, he defeated the army of the state of Qi in eastern China.

Epang Palace: one of the underground complex's palaces.

his burial mound at Mount Li: this section cites Sima Qian's account of the burial mound's construction in *The Historical Records*. It is not clear to what 'sea-people' might refer, although in Japanese this combination of Chinese characters is now used for 'mermen' and 'mermaids'. Mount Li lies northeast of Xi'an in Shaanxi Province.

When I rub my hips on the pine's roots: this alludes to a passage in the nō play *Takasago*, in which the Sumiyoshi deity and the chorus sing: 'Go to a pine's stout root, rub your hips on it, / and a thousand years' fresh green brims from your hands' (Royall Tyler's translation).

Fusang: a mythical land to the east of China in which Penglai was located, sometimes associated with Japan.

the Langya plateau: a plateau near the eastern coast once visited by the First Emperor.

THANKS

The translators would like to thank Naka Tarō's widow, Fukuda Haruko, for her kind permission to publish these translations, Paul Rossiter for his generous and untiring assistance in editing them and seeing them to print, and Peter Robinson, Sam Morrish and Anuradha Gupta for taking the time to read through the translations before publication.

AUTHOR & TRANSLATORS

Naka Tarō (1922-2014) was born Fukuda Shōjirō in Hakata, on the island of Kyūshū in western Japan. He entered Tokyo Imperial University in 1941 to study Japanese Literature but was called up to serve in the Japanese navy in October 1943. His first collection, *Etudes*, was published in 1950; his first mature collection, *Music* (1965), received the Yomiuri and Murō Saisei prizes. He published four further poetry collections: *Hakata* (1975), *No-Self Mountain Temple Diary and Other Poems* (1985), *Excerpts from Travellers of the Dark* (1992), and *Requiems* (1995). His nō play *The First Emperor* was published in 2003 and was performed at the National Noh Theatre in 2014. He also published numerous prose essays and critical works.

Andrew Houwen is a translator of Dutch and Japanese poetry and an associate professor at Tokyo Woman's Christian University. Some of his translations of the Dutch poet Esther Jansma have appeared in *Modern Poetry in Translation* and *Shearsman*.

Chikako Nihei has recently completed a doctoral thesis on the novels of Haruki Murakami at the University of Sydney. She is a lecturer at Yamaguchi University in Japan and is working on a publication concerning Murakami and literary translation.